CHANGED LIVES
MIRACLES
OF THE
PASSION

JODY ELDRED

HARVEST HOUSE PUBLISHERS

EUGENE, OREGON

CHANGED LIVES—MIRACLES OF THE PASSION
Copyright © 2004 by Jody Eldred
Published by Harvest House Publishers
Eugene, Oregon 97402

Library of Congress Cataloging-in-Publication Data

Eldred, Jody, 1956-
  Changed lives—miracles of the passion / Jody Eldred.
    p. cm.
  ISBN 0-7369-1591-5 (pbk.)
  1. Miracles. 2. Spiritual healing. 3. Passion of the Christ (Motion picture) I. Title.
  BT97.3.E43 2004
  231.7'3—dc22   2004018290

Printed in the United States of America.

05 06 07 08 09 10 11 12 / BP-MS / 10 9 8 7 6 5 4 3

Though there are many people in my life
who have greatly impacted my
eternal destiny—my mother, Barbara,
and my early mentors and encouragers,
Ed Gouedy and Joe Carlisle—this book is dedicated
to the One who paid the inestimable price
to secure that destiny for each one of us.

CONTENTS

Introduction   7

Witnessing Miracles
More Than a Movie   17

Tearing Down the Fences
The Reconciliation   27

Believing the Impossible Is Possible
By His Stripes We Are Healed   49

Second Chances
A New Life   67

Miracles Behind the Scenes
Lightning Boy   85
Jim Caviezel   93
All for This 103

180-Degree Turnaround
The God-Hater 111

Doing the Right Thing
Texas Passion Case 135
The Rescue 147

Freedom
There Were Three Crosses 155

Fade to White 171

INTRODUCTION

When God tells you to do something, it's a good idea to do it. And be prepared for war.

It's not very often that I have a clear impression from God that He has something specific He wants me to do. For me, hearing His voice is usually more generic or obvious. ("You have some money—go buy that homeless guy a sandwich.") I believe He speaks clearly, but I think I don't always hear Him clearly because of all the noise and racket in my life.

On January 10, 2004, it must have been very quiet. Or God was speaking very loudly.

Steve McEveety was the executive producer of Mel Gibson's phenomenon, *The Passion of the Christ*. Steve was speaking at a men's gathering early that Saturday morning at Bel Air Presbyterian Church in Los Angeles. Because we'd all heard stories in the press about the film, its controversy, and its realism and violence (guy stuff), the place was packed. In front was a man who was going to show us a clip and then tell us first-hand what it was like making the film. We couldn't wait.

The clip was riveting and moving. I was stunned. Then Steve, in his quiet, unassuming, and still somewhat slightly mystified state, began sharing stories of miraculous occurrences during the filming which clearly indicated God was up to something: an epileptic girl was healed of seizures…a Muslim actor portraying one of the sadistic Roman guards who beat Jesus was now a Christian…a production assistant was struck by lightning *twice* and is perfectly fine…a rebellious Mel Gibson experienced spiritual transformation.

In a moment I knew God was indeed up to something big—something I'd never seen before in my 30 plus years in the TV and film business.

I took a scrap of paper and quickly scribbled on it "TV doc. about changed lives from the film" and showed it to my screenwriter buddy Michael sitting beside me. He read it and then looked me in the eye, nodding with strong affirmation. He knew I was on to something.

After the meeting I chased down McEveety as he was walking to his car (a very Hollywood thing, but I had to). I shared with him my idea and told him I'd been invited to a special screening of the film that night with some potential investors (of which I certainly was *not* one). He thought the idea was intriguing and asked me to call him after the screening to let me know how it went.

The film was overwhelming. I was determined not to like it or be moved by it just because I had high expectations or because, for gosh sakes, I am a Christian. But it was incredible. I was speechless. And in an instant I knew that what God had told me that morning was exactly what I had to do: go find and tell the stories of people whose lives have been miraculously changed by an encounter with the living God through seeing *The Passion of the Christ.*

The next days were filled with a crazy rush to find a way to do this. The movie was coming out in a few weeks; the buzz was building. I needed to shoot opening day, and I knew there would be hundreds of thousands or maybe millions of people incredibly impacted by the film. We would need to find them, tell their stories, and get those stories into a documentary that I wanted on the air by Easter, a few weeks after the film opened.

What was I thinking?

A project like this would usually take months and hundreds of thousands of dollars—and I had neither that kind of time nor that kind of money. But when God tells you to do something, failure is not an option. So off I went. I felt as though I were running toward a cliff with a smile on my face and God was going to catch me when I jumped off.

Which He did, of course. But it was still the hardest thing I've ever done.

As a documentary filmmaker and journalist, I've learned to work very, very fast under really scary deadlines. I thrive in that environment, actually. So this would be another mad dash to the finish line. I'd surround myself with the best and fastest producers and crew I knew…and I knew a lot of them. Seasoned journalists, field producers, cameramen, soundmen, and editors who knew what I was looking for and would go get it, bring it back, slam it together into compelling television, and make it happen—on time.

And these were my friends. We'd dreamed of doing something in our business that really matters. Sure, we'd done hundreds of stories for shows such as *20/20, Primetime, Dateline, 60 Minutes, 48 Hours, World News Tonight, Good Morning America,* and *The Today Show,* but rarely did we have the opportunity to tell stories of people whose eternal destinies had been miraculously rerouted—and because of a movie! This was going to be great.

Oh, yeah…the money. TV is very expensive. We had crews flying all over the country with expenses involving hotels, airfare, rental cars, per diem, and equipment rentals ($1500 a day on the high-definition camera alone). Then there was editing, producer's daily rates to put together the segments, original music to be composed, graphics, attorney fees for contracts and legal/business affairs, insurance…

So I did what any good American who owns a home does. I took out a second mortgage.

What was I thinking?

I've worked with Diane Sawyer quite a bit at ABC News. During the war in the Persian Gulf in 2003, I shot all her stories. We spent some time in sealed shelters wearing gas masks while missiles possibly armed with deadly chemical or biological weapons exploded overhead. It was a stressful experience but good for building camaraderie.

Diane and I also spent several hours together at the Academy Awards in February. I'd agreed to work the Oscars for ABC before I had this crazy idea to do this documentary about changed lives, and we were deep into editing my show and were shooting the last segments. I really didn't have time for it, but I'd made a commitment to them.

Diane's compelling interview with Mel Gibson had just aired on *Primetime.*

We had some down time on our shoot, so we had time to talk about the interview and about the TV special/documentary I was doing. She was particularly intrigued with a bit of technology I was employing that ABC had used in the Persian Gulf. I had received permission from Icon (Mel Gibson's company), the theater, and the audience to take a night-vision camera like we used in the war into the theater and film people's faces as they watched the movie. As far as I know, that had never been done before—certainly not in high-definition.

My camera captured lots of men and women crying or covering their eyes. Some jumped out of their seats (literally). Some sat in shocked, stunned silence. I could see transformation beginning to touch people right then and there. It was truly something to behold. I was quite emotional shooting it, and I felt that emotion again recounting the experience to Diane.

My tireless crews were in the field, trying to get from one city to the next under incredible deadlines. Luggage and equipment lost, flights delayed and canceled, critical interview subjects unavailable on the only day we can be in their city, dead-tired crews arriving at their hotel at midnight to find no reservations and no rooms available, a producer sent to one airport while the crew is waiting for her at another airport in another city. It was a circus of mayhem and I was the ringmaster,

working 18-hour days in editing, writing, directing the host segments, negotiating contracts and deals, managing interpersonal
conflicts, carrying spare cell phone batteries to handle the 100
plus calls each day, and seeing my bank account being depleted
like the gas tank of an SUV flooring it trying to make it up
Mount Everest.

But we were getting terrific interviews, great footage, and
truly compelling stories. When it all came together, the documentary was really firing on all cylinders. We knew this was
going to be something special. And we weren't alone.

Amid another frenetic afternoon an unexpected but wel-
comed phone call came from Diane Sawyer's office. They were
considering doing a piece about "Changed Lives" on *Good
Morning America* and wanted to know if I'd be interested.

"Sure," I calmly replied. I was calm on the outside anyway.

I went back to my editing tasks, thinking about the possibility of sharing these powerful stories about Jesus with a nation.

Two hours later my cell phone rang again.

They wanted me the next day.

"I'll be there."

I was doing my best "this is truly excellent but I'm going to
act very calm as to not appear too excited" routine. After all,
doesn't God do miracles like this? Why should I be so surprised?

That night I finished editing around 10:00, drove home, and
slept for three hours. A limo was scheduled to pick me up at
2:00 A.M. to take me to the ABC affiliate in Hollywood where
I'd do the live interview via satellite. I'd shot dozens of these
interviews for *GMA*, but this time the camera would be on me.

It was a terrific experience. They ran a clip from "By His Stripes," one of the amazing stories you will read in this book. It is a story of prayer, miraculous healing, and God's faithfulness, and I was the lucky guy who got to tell millions of Americans what God was up to—saving lives, transforming lives. And all because of a "coincidental" evening with Diane Sawyer a few weeks prior.

God was clearly up to something here.

Then we were hot property. The phone really started ringing. Joe Scarborough, host of MSNBC's *Scarborough Country,* was next in line. I was on that same night, running the clip of the resurrected baby story and talking about how God is changing lives through *The Passion.* Then CNN was calling, newspapers, the Associated Press, even *The National Inquirer.* The Crystal Cathedral called and wanted me for their internationally broadcast *Hour of Power.* I became an "expert" on changed lives, at least in their eyes. It was a role I was happy to fill.

God's hand was clearly on us. The battle was terrific, and we were exhausted every day well before our work was done, but God's strong arms held us up and provided everything we needed to complete our task. It was the most difficult thing I've ever done, and the most rewarding.

Those two things seem to go hand in hand in my world.

Shortly after the show was finished, I had sent a copy over to Icon Films to get their approval for the film clips I had licensed to use in the broadcast version of our show. My phone rang around 6:00 P.M. It was Steve McEveety and Mel Gibson.

Having briefly met Mel once, 19 years ago, this conversation felt a bit surreal yet at the same time strangely natural. Our mutual excitement for the testimonies in the documentary and the amazing things God was doing through *The Passion of the Christ* turned what could have been a typical Hollywood, all-business conversation into a time of sharing between some heavy hitters and me.

For the next half hour we chatted about the various stories and what they liked most, what most moved them. Mel particularly liked the home videos at the end. He was curious how many stories were out there like the ones I had gathered.

"Based on our research, I'd say about 70,000."

There was a pause in the conversation.

The gravity of such a number struck us all. Seventy thousand. And the film had been out only a few weeks.

"Yes, Mel, the stories are unending."

This book tells just a few of those. They are true stories of real miracles. Real people who have been changed forever by the power of God through *The Passion of the Christ*.

The message is this: Whoever you are, wherever you are, God can reach into your circumstances and make everything new.

All it takes is giving Him a chance to do it.

Just be prepared to be surprised at what He does.

—Jody Eldred
EXECUTIVE PRODUCER
"CHANGED LIVES: MIRACLES OF THE PASSION"

WITNESSING MIRACLES

MORE THAN A MOVIE

What are miracles, really?

I consider myself an expert on miracles in much the same way I am an expert on chocolate.

I have never made chocolate, and rarely cook with it, but I sure have eaten a lot of it. I can tell you in an instant—even by smell—if it's dark chocolate (semi-sweet) or milk chocolate. And by judging how quickly it melts in my mouth I can guess how expensive it is. I don't know what the chemical formulas for various chocolates are, and I don't even know where they're made (only where they're sold!). But in terms of experience, I know chocolate.

As I am not much of a professional cook, I am not much of a professional theologian. But I have consumed a lot of theology over the years. And when it comes to miracles, I have been immersed in them since seeing *The Passion of the Christ*. And even before then. In terms of experience, I know miracles.

As a TV journalist and cameraman for 30 years, I've been in some rough spots: being chased during the L.A. riots, covering the war in Iraq, rescuing a drowning man while working as an underwater photographer, being threatened by armed former Khmer Rouge in Cambodia in remote areas where they'd never find my body, being way too close to explosions that could easily have killed or seriously injured me—and many other dangerous instances known only to God. But I'm still here, all in one piece.

Bravery? Luck? Coincidence?

I can clearly see many times where God reached down from heaven into my circumstances and made something happen that otherwise wouldn't have. Other times He kept something *from* happening that otherwise might have, and I am alive today to proclaim that.

I call those moments miracles. There's no doubt in my mind.

Sure, others can argue, "That wasn't really a miracle…it just worked out that way." Well, from the outside I suppose you could conjecture all kinds of things. But when you are faced with a life-or-death circumstance you have no control over, and you see and feel the protecting hand of God reaching down, grabbing you by the scruff of your neck, and saving your skin, you have no doubt as to the source of your help.

I have heard it said that "a man with only an argument is no match against a man with an experience." I firmly believe that every person sharing a story in this book would agree.

Miracles from a Movie?

In nearly every interview I've done about "Changed Lives," in every television appearance I've made, I am asked this question: Can a movie really cause miracles?

The answer is simple: Nope. A movie can't cause miracles. Only God can do that.

Then how can you say *The Passion of the Christ* has been responsible for all these miracles?

That's the real question, my friend.

No movie can cause a miracle. Neither can a book, a preacher, a shaman, or a golden calf. There's only one source of miracles in the universe, and that is God Himself, the One who died that all mankind might be free, have life, and have it more abundantly.

If you're a skeptic, stay with me here...

I like how my friend Lee Strobel puts it (Lee's an attorney, former journalist, former atheist, and bestselling author):

> You know, *Braveheart* is a motion picture that moved a lot of people. And people had an emotional reaction to it. Did it change lives? I don't think so. Why not? Because it's not based on a historic event that can transform a human being's eternal destiny. It's not based on the truth of what the gospel records, that when we embrace it and when we meet Jesus personally, transforms our entire life, our entire way of thinking, all of our relationships, our priorities, our philosophy, our values, and opens the door of heaven. So there's power that comes with this film because it is based on actual historic truth.

What's the deal with the movie? It's simply a vehicle.

There has never been a film phenomenon like *The Passion of the Christ*. Though radio dramas and movies have affected people for a generation (for example, the famous "War of the

Worlds" radio broadcast sent a nation into a panic), this film
is bringing peace, reconciliation, and miracles to tens of millions of people who are seeing it. There truly has never been
anything like this before.

The stories are amazing—and there are thousands of them
from across the globe. In the pages of this book, I share
accounts from people I directly interviewed about their personal miracles alongside "In Their Own Words"—stories
selected from those thousands gathered via the Internet and
home video submissions. While some of these are anonymous
submissions, others indicate how this film has touched
people from all regions of the United States and the world. They
tell us of lives saved, marriages restored, rescues from addiction, atheists turning their hearts to a God they once hated or
believed didn't exist, a resurrected baby, a murderer who saw
the film and then turned himself in. These incredible stories
tell us about lives that have been forever changed by the power
of God through *The Passion of the Christ.*

The Passion is a lot more than just a movie. It's more than
something that makes you sad or shocked or overcome with
feelings. God is in it. People who see the film are experiencing
something that very few films can offer: the supernatural presence of the real God who really did die a terrible death—will-
ingly—for you and for me. As many people say, "It isn't a movie
you go see, it is a movie you experience."

You might have seen the night-vision footage in my documentary. I took the same night-vision equipment we used at
ABC News covering the Persian Gulf wars, attached it to my
high-definition camera, and with the audience's permission,
recorded their faces as they attended viewings of *The Passion
of the Christ* on opening weekend.

I had seen the film twice already and had a good idea of what was coming. But it was still overwhelming. As I trained the camera on faces all over the theater, and as those now-famous brutal flogging scenes began, nearly every person in the 500-seat theater began to weep. Many covered their eyes, barely peeking out through their fingers. I'd never seen anything like it.

I flashed back a few weeks to that small screening when I first saw the film. My girlfriend sat next to me covering her eyes, crying, hurting, grieving. I remember turning to her, choking back tears myself, and whispering, "You *must* watch." Here was Jesus in the process of redeeming the world, paying the incredibly high price for my disobedience to God. I had to watch. I had to see the price He paid. I had never really known before.

So there in this theater in Burbank, California, 500 people sat, each being touched differently as they experienced what Jesus did for them. I recorded the faces of people who would be beginning new lives. I saw people being set free. My eyes, blurred by my own tears, had difficulty capturing those images. Thirty years as a newsman were of little use as I tried to "just do my job" and emotionally disassociate myself from the experience. God's presence there was overwhelming and irresistible. No one there—including myself—would ever be quite the same. It was an incredible experience I will never forget.

Every time I preach or speak about the cross, the things
I saw on the screen will be on my heart and mind.
—BILLY GRAHAM

Ask anyone who has been radically and forever changed by God whether or not He is real. There is no doubt in their mind. The folks in the following pages will tell you that they experienced *The Passion of the Christ*, and, as a result, they opened themselves up to the possibilities God had for them. God performed a miracle in their lives, and they are very different people as a result—and gratefully so.

God is still in the miracle business. Just as He separated the Red Sea so the Israelites could escape Pharaoh's army, He still provides a way of escape today. Just as Jesus spoke to a man named Lazarus, who'd been dead and decomposing for three days—and Lazarus came back to life—He is bringing back to life those things that we think are dead and hopeless. He is still healing the sick, restoring relationships, bringing peace into violent situations, and, yes, raising the dead.

No matter who you are, no matter what your circumstances may be, no matter how bad life is, you are well within the long reach of God's loving arms.

He's made miracles for me, and He has miracles for you too.

The Power of Passion

The title of the film hinges on the word "passion." When we speak of "miracles of the Passion"—there it is again. It's a curious use of a word we know well. Or do we?

I have passion for several things. You already know one of them: chocolate! I also have a passion for the underwater world, as I've been a SCUBA diver for over 20 years. I don't have a passion for all cats, but I have a passion for my cat ("Knucklehead," an affectionate name). I have passion for America, passion for truth, and passion for orphans in Cambodia. I have passion for God.

God's passion for us is quite different from anything we have passion for. In fact, the word itself takes on an entirely different meaning that is only barely related to the deep feelings we passionately hold.

Catholic Archbishop Charles J. Chaput describes it this way. "The Latin word *passio* from which the English word 'passion' comes, means 'to suffer.' The original meaning of the Latin root for the word is 'to endure, to suffer, to bear a heavy burden.'"

Is it coming into focus for you now?

Yes, "passion" does retain its meaning of strong feelings directed toward a person or an object you cherish and treasure. But when the word comes from God and is directed toward you and me, there is so much more meaning poured into it.

The passion of Christ is depicted quite accurately (and brutally) in *The Passion of the Christ*. He suffered. He endured. He bore a very heavy burden. And He did it because of His passion for us.

So when we speak of "miracles of the Passion," we speak of supernatural life-changes as a result of seeing Mel Gibson's film. But more importantly, we speak of incredible, true miracles that have happened because of that suffering, that heavy burden, that endurance, that man—Jesus.

These are the miracles of His passion.

> *We need to see what happened*
> *in the death of Jesus for two reasons.*
> *To see His passion for us but to*
> *awaken our passion for Him.*
> —JACK HAYFORD

SURVEY SAYS: CHANGED LIVES

Mel Gibson's controversial movie about the last 12 hours of the life of Jesus, *The Passion of the Christ,* stunned the movie industry by becoming the eighth highest-grossing domestic film of all-time.

A new national survey of more than 1600 adults, conducted by the Barna Group, examines not only how many people saw the movie, but what impact the film had on their life.

People who had seen *The Passion* were asked if it affected their religious beliefs in any way. When pressed to describe the specific shifts in their spiritual perspectives, the most common changes were the perceived importance of how they treat other people, becoming more concerned about the affect of their life choices and personal behavior, and gaining a deeper understanding of, or appreciation for, what Christ had done for them through His death and resurrection.

The Passion was well received and stopped many people long enough to cause them to rethink some of their basic assumptions about life.

Barna also highlighted the power of movies in transforming people's lives. "Don't lose sight of the fact that about 13 million adults changed some aspect of their typical religious behavior because of the movie and about 11 million people altered some pre-existing religious beliefs because of the content of that film. That's enormous influence," the California-based researcher noted, "and you cannot fault *The Passion* for not satisfying religious agendas that some people assigned to it. More than any other movie in recent years, *The Passion* focused people on the person and purpose of Jesus Christ. In a society that revolves on relativism, spiritual diversity, tolerance and independence, galvanizing such intense consideration of Jesus Christ is a major achievement in itself."*

---

* Taken from "The Barna Update," July 10, 2004. Copyright © 2004 The Barna Group, www.barna.org. Used with permission.

TEARING DOWN THE FENCES

THE RECONCILIATION

"It is a phenomenal thing. I really think God is using Mel Gibson in ways he never expected."

That's what James Morrison has to say about

how *The Passion of the Christ* worked a miracle of reconciliation in his own life. This is an incredible story of "bad blood" and violence between an employer (James) and two employees (Alex and Anthony Scott) turning into genuine forgiveness and understanding. This is a story of three men forever changed by the power of *The Passion*.

CHANGED LIVES

There's a small town in the windy panhandle of Texas called Borger. The pivotal day in July 2003 started out like so many others for James Morrison. As the administrator of the town's nursing home, James conducted employee evaluations. Today he was meeting with employee Wilma Scott, the dietary services manager of the food service department. Up until a few weeks prior, both of Wilma's sons, Alex and Anthony, had also been employed at the nursing home.

James is an educated, soft-spoken administrator. In contrast, Wilma's two boys were young laborers, neither well educated, nor well spoken. The brothers were known for being rough around the edges and violent; they were a bit proud of this reputation. There was a lot of hate inside them.

Things had not gone well when Anthony had been working at the nursing home with his mother and Alex. James had had to let Anthony go because of his poor job performance just a week before his mother's performance evaluation.

That did not sit well with a young man prone to violence.

With tension and hard feelings already stirring within the Scott family, James knew that his morning meeting with Wilma would be stressful because the evaluation he prepared for her was not favorable.

It was the setting for a perfect storm. After receiving her negative evaluation, Wilma left work in the middle of the day, needing time and some distance to decide whether she would look for another job. Once she told Alex and Anthony her news, the storm was unleashed.

Alex Scott

It made us mad. It made my brother a lot more mad than it made me. Anthony said he had to go talk to James, and then he set outta here real quick. I pleaded for him to come back home because I knew there was going to be some trouble.

Wilma Scott

Anthony told me he was going to talk to James, and I said, "Don't." But after I left he went ahead anyway.

Anthony Scott

My mom told me not to go over to the nursing home because she knew I was a very cruel person. I was known for fighting and for getting real angry.

Alex

We'd worked at the kitchen at the care center under James Morrison. And none of us got along with James.

As soon as Wilma left the house, Anthony took off for the nursing home with Alex close behind.

Alex

We went over there to confront James. Just to let him know we were upset about our mother's evaluation and that we didn't think it was fair.

Anthony

Well, I went over to the nursing home with my brother, but James hadn't made it there yet. I wanted to get my brother out of there before anything happened, but before I can, James shows up.

After his meeting with Wilma, James had spent the rest of the morning and early afternoon seeing physicians around town, alerting them to the head count and bed availability at the nursing home. Around mid-afternoon, James drove back into the nursing home parking lot to find Anthony and Alex waiting for him.

James Morrison

The two sons were waiting for me when I pulled up into the parking lot.

When I got out of the car, Anthony ran towards me and starting pushing off on me.

Anthony

I walked up to him, and I was angry. I asked him, "Why'd you give my mom a bad evaluation?"

James tried to appeal to logic and reason, hoping they could handle this as adults. It wasn't working.

James

I told Anthony it was between his mom and me, but he continued to mouth off.

In Anthony's one-track mind, his mama had been done wrong, and there was no turning back.

Alex

James and Anthony went back and forth for a minute, and then James said, "This is none of your business." After that, Anthony swung at him, hitting him in the jaw.

It was a strong punch from a man who'd hit many people. James' glasses went flying. Stunned, he fell forward trying to grab a light post to keep from hitting the ground.

James

I was completely caught off guard when Anthony hit me with a left hook.

Alex

He hugged a post 'cause I'm sure his knees were about to buckle. Anthony...he hit hard.

James Morrison is not a fighter. He'd never been hit like that—and never saw it coming. But he did see big Alex moving in his direction.

James
> Out of my peripheral vision I saw Alex get up from the patio and rush toward me.

Alex was ready to rumble. Filled with rage and wanting to avenge his mother's pain, he raced into the action against his employer—but fortunately for James, Alex's rage was confined to language. Before the brothers left, Alex told James that he quit. That was unnecessary, of course....

As the Scott boys walked away, James knew something was very wrong with him. He was in serious pain and his face was swollen like a grapefruit. But full of anger—and fear—he first went to the police and filed assault charges. Hours later he found himself in an emergency room in Amarillo, looking at X-rays and hearing the news that his jaw had been seriously broken.

For the next six weeks—maybe longer—his jaw would have to be wired shut, and he would be eating his food through a straw. This was a severe injury.

Time passed and his jaw slowly began to heal, but James' heart was getting worse. Fear, anger, and the desire for revenge was taking root. The pastor at his church, Dr. Paul Anderson, saw it up close.

Pastor Anderson

James was badly hurt. At the same time, he had a fear of these guys. He had a fear of what they might to do him again.

James

I told the business office manager that if Wilma came back, she was fired. In fact, she did come back to the nursing home that day, learned what had happened, and was let go. When I got back from the hospital from having all of the medical work done, I installed dead bolts on my doors.

Living in a small town made it particularly challenging for James. Driving to and from work required him to pass by Alex

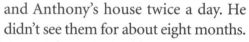 and Anthony's house twice a day. He didn't see them for about eight months.

But they saw him.

Alex spent time shooting hoops at the house and sitting around. From his front porch he'd stare at every car going by to see if one might be James Morrison's. He was hoping James would see him and be scared that something else bad would happen.

Alex was full of hate, and James was full of fear and unforgiveness. They were both confined to prisons of their own making.

James

I had some anxiety, some frustration. I had some anger. Because I had been assaulted, I wanted for there to be justice. Anthony received "deferred adjudication," meaning that if he didn't get into trouble again, the assault charges go away. But I wanted Anthony to go to jail for what he had done. The police told me to call if I ever felt threatened again by either Anthony or Alex, but I never saw them again.

I didn't feel that the whole matter had been resolved. I was mad because I didn't think I did anything wrong [regarding Wilma Scott].

At Wilma's home, the situation wasn't any better. The brothers' anger and frustration toward James were turning into hatred.

Anthony

At the time [of the assault] I didn't care about James. As soon as I left him, I was laughing! Me and my brother joked around because James collapsed.

Alex

I blamed James for everything that happened. My mom was out of work, I was out of work, my brother was in trouble with the law. We were paying fines and weren't making much money at the time. I had a lot of hatred in me for the man. I wanted to hurt him.

Wilma

Anthony told me that he really didn't want to get into an altercation. I lost my job, and he had a lot of guilt over that because he knew fighting wasn't the way to handle things.

Eight months goes by. James' jaw is almost healed, but his heart still aches as fear and unforgiveness lingers and consumes.

Anthony finds work on a road construction crew—tough work in Texas weather extremes. Alex still has no job.

They are both unrepentant, unhappy, unfulfilled. Still impris-
oned by their anger and hardened hearts.

But a miracle is on the way.

A film phenomenon comes to Borger: *The Passion of the
Christ*. None of the huge international press and potential controversy is lost on this small town. James Morrison and his friend
Dr. Steve Elston are in line opening night. Not only is Dr. Elston
a friend of James, but he is a local physician and knows how
much physical and emotional pain remains for James.

As the friends buy their tickets and walk into the lobby,
James catches a glimpse of the last people in the world he
expects to be at the film…

James

I had forgiven Alex and Anthony the best that I could; I really
thought the whole thing was out of my mind by this time. Yet when
Steve and I went into the foyer of the theater, we saw Wilma and
Alex there. They saw me too, but we didn't say anything to each
other. Once inside the theater itself, Steve and I sat on one side
and they sat on the other.

Tension was building. Old wounds were opening up. "Why
does this have to happen?" It was shaping up to be a bad night
for James Morrison.

So he thought.

Dr. Elston

Before the movie started, James pointed out to me the brother
of the man who had beaten him up last year. I knew that seeing

that young man made James uncomfortable—it was kind of a sore spot with him because James felt he never got satisfaction through the legal system. I think he felt vulnerable…as if something could happen again.

James

When we got into our seats, I started praying. I had read about the awesome effect this movie was having on people. I prayed that God would touch Alex and Wilma, that they would be affected by this movie.

I also realized that I was still hurt and angry about the whole thing. I was still harboring vindictive thoughts about wanting to get even.

James didn't know it, but Alex was having a few thoughts of his own.

Alex

When James came into the theater, I started cussing under my breath because I didn't want to see him.

The lights went down, the movie began, and the miracle started to take form.

James

As I watched the movie, I became torn up inside. I was mournful, sad. As a Christian I had known intellectually what had happened to Christ on the cross, but to see it depicted on the screen brought the whole experience to life. I could hardly put into words what Christ had done for us. After the movie ended, there was such silence in the theater.

I couldn't say anything; I was so stunned.

James wasn't the only one.

The scenes of Jesus' flogging and brutal execution played on the screen, but the reality of what Jesus endured was imprinting on Alex's soul too. It was unlike anything he'd ever experienced.

Alex

As I was watching *The Passion of the Christ*, I felt as though I wasn't in the theater at all. I was there, watching what actually happened to Jesus.

Suddenly, these feelings started coming over me, and I knew I needed to get this hate out of my heart.

When the credits started rolling at the end of the movie, I knew I had to go make peace with James.

But James and Steve had left the theater quickly and were walking toward their car. They wanted no contact with Alex or Wilma. Then James heard someone calling out for him.

"James...James..."

He turned around and there was Alex Scott, running out of the theater toward him—with tears in his eyes.

James

We were outside on the sidewalk when I heard my name. It was Alex, coming after me.

Dr. Elston

When Alex had caught up with us, you could tell that he was really shaken up.

James

Alex came up from behind me; I was initially apprehensive. Then, as he held out his hand, I saw that he was crying. He said how sorry he was again and again.

Alex

I said, "I…I just want to make peace with you." I shook his hand and hugged him. About that time I started crying real bad. I just told him "I'm sorry, I'm sorry" several times.

Alex's heart, hardened over from years of hatred, anger, and unforgiveness, had been broken—and mended—through the power of *The Passion*. A true miracle.

James

Wow! I couldn't believe it. What a big step for Alex to make. How humbling it must have been for him. Here he is, this kid who wanted to be a gangbanger. It was really amazing.

We shook hands; we hugged. I told him I forgave him. At that moment a completely new sense of wholeness came over me.

A smiling Alex Scott recounted his experience and the joy and peace he now felt—for the first time.

Alex

I've seen the movie twice since then. It's not like you are watching a movie on the screen; it's as though you are experiencing it yourself. *The Passion* helped me to understand how hate had consumed me.

Now, I'm free. It's as though I have been released from prison! Makes me want to do better. To be a better man.

When I told my mom about making peace with James, she was so happy we both cried.

Like Alex, James was a new man too. A few weeks later, he saw Alex, his girlfriend, and Wilma Scott at a local restaurant. But this time, instead of fear or anger, James' heart was changed. He went over to their table and shook hands with his former enemy, who received him as a friend.

It was a miracle to James. He could hardly believe the change—in Alex and in himself. But there was still Anthony Scott—the brother who had actually broken his jaw. He was just as mean and violent as ever.

James

I was really astounded. When all this started happening, I went to Alex's house to talk to him. Anthony was in the parking lot; he told me to get my a** off his property.

Alex

Anthony wasn't having it. He was prone to violence. I mean, he was always hitting somebody.

Anthony

I hated James. I was a very cruel person. I fought just because I wanted to, really. I mean, I didn't have to hit James…

With the transformation of heart that Alex was experiencing, it wasn't long before he tried to convince Anthony to go see *The Passion* with him. Anthony seemed like a lost cause, but Alex had hope.

Anthony finally agreed to see it, and the long reach of God's love extended right to the theater seat where Anthony sat. It was inescapable.

Anthony

During *The Passion of the Christ* what hit me toward the end was where they are crucifying Christ. You just see that teardrop, coming from above, like the last breath of His life. That affected me very emotionally. I was in tears.

Anthony was convicted that his life wasn't right and that his life wasn't working. Here was Jesus—an innocent man of peace—being horribly beaten and killed, and God Himself shed a tear when He died. Anthony knew right then that he had to try another way of living.

There in that theater his heart was broken. Anthony Scott felt God's incredible love for him like never before. For the first time, he decided he must find the good plan that God had for his life. Change was stirring in him.

Anthony

When Alex told me that he had made peace with James, I told him he had done a good thing and that maybe someday I would be able to do that too.

Could it be true? Was a reconciliation between the boss and the man who'd broken his jaw possible?

That opportunity soon arrived through an unexpected route; a posting on the Internet and a phone call from someone he had never met.

The day after hearing about the incredible story of Alex's reconciliation with James from her husband Steve, Martha

Elston discovered a website, MyLifeAfter.com, where movie-goers from around the world post stories about how *The Passion* has changed their lives. Martha submitted the story of Alex and James' reconciliation and closed by writing, "My husband said that in knowing the facts of what had happened and a little of the basics about the incident, he considered what he had witnessed an act of God."

It wasn't long after Martha's posting that Anthony received a telephone call from one of the producers of the TV special, "Changed Lives: Miracles of the Passion." Anthony agreed to meet James with the camera rolling; it would be the first time the men would speak since the incident almost a year earlier.

In a few days, the previously unthinkable happened. With

outstretched hands, the two men found peace with one another.

James boldly strode onto the property where he'd last been obscenely ordered off, and out came a smiling Anthony Scott, his hand extended.

Anthony

How's it goin', James?

James

Hey man, it's good.

Anthony

I just thought we'd call it over with.

James

I know this is tough for you. I know it's not easy.

Anthony

I don't fight no more. I don't do none of that. I'm grown up more. I guess I'm becoming an adult…

The two men stood outside and visited for 20 minutes like old friends. It was an incredible scene. The lion and the lamb. A reconciliation.

For James, Anthony, and Alex, *The Passion of the Christ* opened their hearts to a new way of living. Anger was replaced by forgiveness. Fear was replaced by love. They are new men from the inside out, transformed by God, who reached out to them in a theater.

Anthony's character has completely changed. His manner has softened, he smiles, and he has an obvious peace in his life he never experienced before—and never knew was waiting for him.

Anthony

The movie touched me in so many ways. I always felt that I was a real violent person.

I had a violent dog; I'd just hit him, and that kind of shows me that I was violent myself. But now I've got fish…and fish are calm. I *never* thought I'd have fish…

Anthony smiles as he reflects on how much he truly has changed.

Anthony

I don't see me being violent no more. I couldn't hit somebody and not care about it. I thank James for actually forgiving me for what I did.

Alex

This movie gave me so much hope.

To the world, the situation for these three men looked hopeless indeed. But to God, nothing was impossible. Because they gave God a chance, James Morrison and Alex and Anthony Scott will never be the same.

CHANGED LIVES ·

My son had been in and out of drug rehabilitation centers for years. Nothing seemed to help. I prayed fervently for him, for I am a devoted follower of Jesus. I took him to see *The Passion,* and the next day he entered rehab again. I did not give it much hope, but he is out and is living a good life free from drugs. I truly believe he will make it this time. Yes, I believe in miracles, and my son is living proof.

—Internet submission

Truly the greatest thing I witnessed was a family that came in together and sat down near me during a matinee showing of *The Passion.* It was my second trip to the movie, so I knew what to expect and was prepared with a washcloth and 25 napkins. They were four brothers and a sister, all in their forties, who came in and sat three seats over from me on my left. You could tell they were all related because they all looked alike. Same red hair, same build.

Three of the brothers were clean-cut, and the other was a huge, tough guy, biker-type. You could tell he had been dragged to the movie and was not happy about being there. He had a long unwashed biker braid, arms full of snake tattoos, and ratty Harley Hog clothes—definitely not a man you would mess with! I knew they had brought him to see the movie because he was not saved. He was the one sitting closest to me, so I began to pray for him. The movie started, and before long I saw him wiping his nose, I prayed harder. Then tears came as they scourged Jesus. He was slumped back in his seat, tough-guy demeanor gone; he was literally undone. Sobs burst forth from him uncontrollably.

After the movie he was totally pale and absolutely limp as a rag. As the credits started to roll, his sister fell, weeping like Mary Magdelene, down on the theater floor in front of him as she literally begged him to give his life to Jesus. He bent over her, reached out and grabbed her hand, and was broken and sobbing...they were all sobbing together...we were all sobbing...the whole place sobbed together and rejoiced!

I know that I witnessed God break through to that man's heart right then. The abandoned compassion of his sister as she knelt and begged her brother to give his life to the Lord, and his broken response, I will never forget. It was one of the greatest things I have ever seen! This movie set that atmosphere and allowed the Holy Spirit to work in this man's heart to bring him to salvation. He will never be the same again...and I know I will never be the same again, either.

—Internet submission

The movie put my imagination of what [Christ's Passion] was like on a big screen. Most of us already know the story, but while watching the movie, in your own mind you want Jesus to be saved. The movie has changed the way I think of Jesus by making us witness the pain and torture He was put through. No matter how many times we read it, do we really put ourselves there? I didn't until now. It made a bigger impact on my

13-year-old son. Afterward I was explaining how Easter would pick up from where the movie ended. He turned to me and said, "Mom, this movie would be a really big book." I replied, "It already is. It's called the Bible."

—Internet submission

As I watched this story of sacrificial love unfold right before my eyes, I was hit with the stark reality of the magnitude of my sins. The next day, by the grace of God, I went next door and I asked my neighbor to forgive me for the anger and resentment that had built up in my heart toward him.

—Submitted by a former gunnery sergeant
in the U.S. Marine Corps in
Jacksonville, Florida

Two other men, both criminals, were also led out with him to be executed. When they came to the place called the Skull, there they crucified him, along with the criminals—one on his right, the other on his left. Jesus said, "Father, forgive them, for they do not know what they are doing." And they divided up his clothes by casting lots...

One of the criminals who hung there hurled insults at him: "Aren't you the Christ? Save yourself and us!"

But the other criminal rebuked him. "Don't you fear God," he said, "since you are under the same sentence? We are punished justly, for we are getting what our deeds deserve. But this man has done nothing wrong."

Then he said, "Jesus, remember me when you come into your kingdom."

Jesus answered him, "I tell you the truth, today you will be with me in paradise."

LUKE 23:32-34,39-43

BELIEVING THE IMPOSSIBLE IS POSSIBLE

BY HIS STRIPES
WE ARE HEALED

Michael and Krista Branch had been Christians for a long time. They believed that Jesus was who He said He was, and generally speaking, they trusted Him with their lives. They'd taken the opportunity to go see a new film just released, *The Passion of the Christ.*

Michael describes that experience.

CHANGED LIVES

Michael Branch

My wife, Krista, and I went to see *The Passion* opening day, which was a Wednesday. Of course we were very moved by it. The things that we saw put a vision in our minds as to what actually happened—which before was left up to our imaginations—and we didn't know how historically correct we were. We talked about the movie numerous times after we saw it.

Saturday I had a conversation with my brother-in-law, and I told him that what really struck me about the movie was what Mary went through losing her son. And of course the flashback scene when Jesus fell and Mary runs and tells him she's there, and what it must be like to go through the loss of a child.... Literally that conversation was Saturday night.

Then Sunday morning rolls around...

It began as a typical Sunday morning in the Branch home in Divide, Colorado, just outside Colorado Springs. Two of their three small children were in high chairs, having breakfast. Michael was doing a little work at his computer, and Krista had just put 11-month-old Kenna Beth into the tub for a shower.

In a few moments they would learn something about the reality of their faith. Their whole world was about to change.

Michael

We got up this morning like any other Sunday morning. We scurried around the house getting Kalon and Kassidy fed and Krista went up to get Kenna. When she brought her downstairs we saw that she was messy from a runny nose, and so I suggested to Krista that she give Kenna a shower. Krista took her in the bathroom and put her in the bathtub. We usually unscrew the stopper from the tub and all three kids play in the shower together. In the hurriedness of getting ready we neglected to unscrew the stopper and just pulled it out instead. What Krista didn't see was that Kenna had sat on the stopper and pushed it down so that the tub was slowly filling with water.

Krista Branch

I put her in there and washed her all off. I was headed for the towels, and I was about to get her out when she started playing so hard...she was having such a good time.

Michael

I was looking for a website, and I thought Krista could help me, so I yelled for her to come in here and help me for a minute.

Krista

Our computer was acting up and not accessing the website we were looking for, so I stayed for a little bit to try and figure out what the problem was. And of course I was listening to Kenna Beth the whole time…periodically I would go back and make sure she was still playing, make sure she wasn't ready to get out. I was out of the bathroom for perhaps four minutes.

Then I went to the bathroom door and saw water. Immediately my heart sank and I thought, "*Oh, no!*" I ran to the shower and yanked the curtain back and saw her floating face down. I was certain she was dead. I started panicking.

Michael

As you can imagine, Krista screamed hysterically and I knew immediately something was very, very wrong. I jumped up out of my chair and ran in there. As I was hurrying into the bedroom, Krista met me at the door, holding Kenna out face-first to me. I grabbed her at arm's length and held her there for a second, trying to process, you know.

Krista

Michael grabbed her from me and put her on the bed. I guess from being in the position she was…head hanging down, her mouth had been open in the water. Now her mouth had closed, but her tongue was still sticking out a bit over her bottom lip. She didn't look like my daughter. She just looked very different. I was pretty much sure she was dead. She was gray…didn't have any color at all. Not purple, not blue. Just gray. She looked like a corpse.

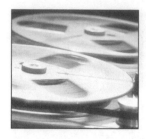

Moments later, Krista made a frantic call to 911.

911 Dispatcher

Teller County 911. Where is your emergency?

Krista

(hysterical)
Ah…my ba-…my…my…

911 Dispatcher

Take a deep breath and tell me what's going on.

Krista

Oh my God. My baby…

911 Dispatcher

Your baby's what?

Krista

She's…she…she's…she was taking a bath. She's not breathing. She's all blue.

911 Dispatcher

Okay, get her to the floor.

Krista

(yelling)
Get her to the floor!

911 Dispatcher

I'm going to tell you what to do, okay?

Jerry Kerr is a veteran detective with the Teller County Sheriff's Department. He was on duty that Sunday morning.

Detective Kerr

What I first heard was that a 911 call was coming over a scanner. I heard the officers receive the call...and overheard that there was a baby involved and unconscious.

Michael

Kenna felt like rubber. There was no life in her. From the moment I touched her, call it a spiritual thing or whatever, I knew she was not in her body...she was gone.

There were no words to express what I was feeling at that moment. There were no words to pray that expressed to God the horror I was experiencing and the fear I was battling against.

From the second I got her I was hearing "It's hopeless," "Prepare for the funeral," and "You're going to be the father of two children now." Maybe if I had heard only one thing I would have bought it. If it had been more subtle...but because it was a barrage of lies, I wanted to say, "How dare you come into my home and try to steal my family?" It was so undeniably in my face that this was an attack, that this was not of God.

I began to groan uncontrollably...I was raised Baptist, so there were not a whole lot of tongue-talkers in my family, but I truly believe this was a case of my spirit groaning in words I could not express, could not pray in my own intellect.

I realized right away that this was an attack of Satan. And it...it wasn't...it didn't *have* to be this way. Yes, there was fault on my wife's and my part, but literally the thief came into my house to steal, kill, and destroy that morning. This is where *The Passion* comes in. I began to have visions—as Krista did—of the flogging scene—so vividly in my mind.

The Scripture "by His stripes we are healed" continued to run through my mind…"the chastisement of our peace was upon Him." Satan was trying to steal our peace; he was trying to destroy our lives; he was trying to steal our daughter away from us and kill every dream or aspiration for her that we have. In that one act, he was trying to utterly destroy us. So that Scripture and those scenes from the movie kept coming to my mind over and over again, the flogging scene…"by His stripes we are healed."

God was saying, "You don't have to take the punishment." By those stripes we have the authority to take back what was ours. I kept having visions of Jesus holding our baby and bringing her back to us. And I began to yell, "You are not going to steal my daughter. You are not going to steal my daughter."

Krista

I too just knew that it was not her time to go, that Jesus had already healed her. So I thanked Him for it.

Her belief in this truth is heard on the 911 call:

Krista

Thank You, Jesus. Thank You, Jesus. Thank You, Jesus…

911 Dispatcher

Okay, I want you to get her to the floor…

In a drowning victim, brain damage will usually occur after four to six minutes. After that, the potential for serious brain damage greatly increases with each passing minute. It is estimated that Kenna Beth Branch was without oxygen for eight to ten minutes—or more.

Detective Kerr, who'd heard the call on his radio, raced to the Branch home. He was the first to arrive.

Detective Kerr

When I looked at the baby, she didn't have any color. I don't know how long she had been without oxygen. She was unconscious. She was very typical of a dead body.

While Kerr and other deputies who'd arrived were attempting to revive Kenna Beth, paramedics had been dispatched and were on the way.

Erin Ewers, a father, is a paramedic had had responded to many emergencies regarding children. They were his most difficult cases.

Paramedic Ewers

It's a call that no paramedic wants to get. A child down, not breathing, CPR in progress. That's really scary stuff, especially when you have kids of your own. Once we got there, the child looked really gray…initially really unresponsive. It was not looking good.

The paramedics continued CPR on little Kenna Beth, not expecting much. There was great fear that she was indeed dead, and if revived, would have serious brain damage.

Detective Kerr

My primary concern once we got her in the ambulance and on oxygen was whether there was going to be some damage to this baby.

They put Kenna Beth in the ambulance and then sped to a nearby schoolyard where a Flight for Life helicopter was waiting to airlift her down the mountain to Memorial Hospital in Colorado Springs.

Michael then picked up the phone and made another call.

John Branch, Kenna's Grandfather

It's one of those phone calls you never want to get. But the phone rang, and when I answered it, Michael said, "Dad, I need you."

I knew from the tone of his voice something terrible had happened. I asked him, "What's wrong?"

He said, "Kenna Beth drowned in the shower."

Paramedics continued to work on the baby, performing CPR and working to insert an IV. They had little hope.

But they were unaware that a power far greater than them was at work in that ambulance.

Michael and Krista had desperately cried out to God to reach into the most dire circumstance a parent can face. They had no other place to turn and believed with all their hearts that the price Jesus paid in dying for them was enough to bring their little girl back.

God heard their plea.

Paramedic Ewers

For some reason she came back really quickly with a little bit of resuscitation. She started to let us know how much she did not approve of us trying to start an IV on her. It actually turned out really well.

By the time the helicopter arrived at Memorial Hospital, Kenna Beth was miraculously breathing on her own and already getting fidgety!

Doctors were concerned about brain damage and performed a CT scan. A short time later they returned with the results.

Michael

Five minutes later the doctor came in and said the CT scan came back normal. He kept saying, "You're lucky. You're lucky. You don't know how lucky you are" as if he was confused that she was doing so well! I don't believe in luck. I believe the Lord brought her back.

People were praying, and so I think that was what really saved her. I leaned over Kenna and whispered in her ear, "Daddy loves you…you're going to be okay. Daddy loves you."

John

Kenna Beth woke up…looked at my son and said, "Dada," and smiled…and at that point he knew he had his little girl back.

No brain damage. The baby revived.
There was no other explanation. A miracle had occurred.

Detective Kerr

Well, they're extremely lucky. To have the opportunity to see them get their girl back was a real thrill for all of us.

John

These kind of miracles take place often. We sometimes don't attribute them to be miracles, but this was the work of God—there's no doubt about that.

Today, Michael and Krista Branch are different people. Different parents. They see life in a new, clearer way. They have experienced Christ's passion for them in an indisputable and unforgettable manner.

And Kenna Beth is a walking miracle.

Michael

There have been no aftereffects. Kenna's perfect—better than ever. She's literally a different baby in a good way. The smiling, the messing around with Mommy and Daddy. She's a lot more personable. It's really strange! It seems as though she's happier.

I hate to think there could have been a different outcome, but because *The Passion of the Christ* was so fresh in our minds, and because of the scenes we saw, the love we saw portrayed in the movie even in the flogging and crucifixion, was so fresh in our hearts, that when this happened, we believed in our minds and hearts that this was an attack and was not suppose to happen...that Jesus already paid this price, and Kenna didn't have to pay it; we didn't have to pay it.

Had this happened a week before I'd seen the movie, I would not have been so on edge and ready to defend my family spiritually. I guess a good way to describe it is how September 11 heightened our awareness of the possibility of terrorist attacks. After I saw this movie, it heightened my awareness of the unimaginable love God has for us—that He'd go through such torment—and it heightened my awareness of the tactics of Satan and attacks of Satan—that he wants to steal, kill, and destroy.

I could have accepted that my daughter was dead, and it would have been a done deal. But in that heightened awareness we recognized the attack and acknowledged that Jesus paid the price. He raised her from the dead. I know she was dead. No doubt in my mind.

Krista

Jesus suffered for this very reason, for such a time as this. I don't know what would have been going through my mind if I had not seen the movie. I wouldn't have had such a confidence in Jesus. That was something that I had personally been dealing with. I'd never really experienced Jesus. I was raised in Christian home and saved at age five. I knew how to act, I knew how to serve Jesus, but He's never been so real to me. *The Passion of the Christ* made you think about the price He really paid. I don't think I would have been so confident about praying for Kenna if I had not had those images in my mind.

Through tear-filled eyes, Kenna's grandfather sums it up beautifully. "We know that God gave our little girl back to us. I haven't heard anyone put it any better than my daughter when she said that the angels took Kenna Beth and hugged her...and then gave her back."

He was wounded for our transgressions,
He was bruised for our iniquities;
The chastisement for our peace was upon Him,
And by His stripes we are healed.

ISAIAH 53:5 NKJV

CHANGED LIVES

The reality is that we are all living in the middle of the war zone of good versus evil. *The Passion* brought that realization home. Watching Satan walk among the crowds made me really aware of the fact that he walks among us every day while trying to separate us from Christ. He does a good job, too, if we let him catch us off guard.

Tina—Riverton, Wyoming

We have been Christians for many years and have seen many miracles that have occurred with changed lives and had healings, but we were not prepared or expecting the Lord to heal my ankle when we went into the movie.

For three days an ankle which I had broken years back was giving out on me. I am 63 years old. I had taken out my crutches and needed them to walk. I couldn't put any weight on it or I would fall. I went out during the movie for a restroom break. I needed the crutches to get out. Coming back I thought, "I can walk. There's not anything wrong with my ankle." I knew right away that God had made it well. I carried the crutches back. My wife gave me a strange look, took the crutches, put them against the wall, and finished watching the movie. We thanked the Lord afterward as we walked out. I know that the Lord is our Savior, provider, healer, friend, and more.

—Internet submission

I was diagnosed with lung cancer about five months ago. My sister and I went to the movie theater and saw *The Passion* together before my surgery, and we were forever changed. My surgery was the following Friday, and our pastor came to pray with us before they wheeled me into the operating room. Two hours later, the surgeon told my family that there was no cancer anywhere inside me! Seeing *The Passion of the Christ* set off a chain of events that led to my sister's and my salvation, and a miracle of God...praise the Lord.

—Milton, Ohio

What I wasn't prepared for was watching Jesus through Mary's eyes. You see, my precious son Michael and his fiancée, Patricia, were killed when a drunk driver crushed them in their car two years ago.

Having a chance to see much from Mary's view broke my heart as I thought about losing Michael. Mary's helplessness to protect her child from His death was overwhelming... especially when she ran to Jesus as He fell under the burden of the cross...and the flashback...so powerful. When she kissed His feet on the cross...that was heart wrenching. The last thing I did before leaving Michael's body in the stark and cold emergency room was hold his feet...what mother doesn't long to hold and caress her baby's precious feet?

Mary and I and every mother who has lost a child is left with only one healing choice. Trusting the Lord and the promises He has given us to stand upon to give us the strength we desperately need to move forward, to accept God's will, and to trust His purpose when we cannot understand.

After the credits rolled I could not leave my seat. Stunned, I could only say, "Thank You, Jesus. Thank You, Jesus. Thank You, Jesus."

—Internet submission

Having watched this film will forever change the way I relate to and read the Gospel accounts. I could not help but be drawn to read them that night. I had an intense new appreciation for that time in history, the way I could relate to Jesus' humanity from the way He chose to suffer and bear the penalty for our sin. I have been overwhelmed with gratitude.

Seeing those 12 hours come alive has still left me speechless. Jesus modeled the most amazing love and grace during His Passion. What a demonstration, what a vivid reminder we will have to help us remember the cost for our redemption.

Linda—Warrington, Pennsylvania

One day as he was teaching, Pharisees and teachers of the law, who had come from every village of Galilee and from Judea and Jerusalem, were sitting there. And the power of the Lord was present for him to heal the sick.

Some men came carrying a paralytic on a mat and tried to take him into the house to lay him before Jesus. When they could not find a way to do this because of the crowd, they went up on the roof and lowered him on his mat through the tiles into the middle of the crowd, right in front of Jesus.

When Jesus saw their faith, he said, "Friend, your sins are forgiven."

The Pharisees and the teachers of the law began thinking to themselves, "Who is this fellow who speaks blasphemy? Who can forgive sins but God alone?"

Jesus knew what they were thinking and asked, "Why are you thinking these things in your hearts? Which is easier: to say, 'Your sins are forgiven,' or to say, 'Get up and walk'? But that you may know that the Son of Man has authority on earth to forgive sins...." *He said to the paralyzed man, "I tell you, get up, take your mat and go home."*

Immediately he stood up in front of them, took what he had been lying on and went home praising God. Everyone was amazed and gave praise to God. They were filled with awe and said, "We have seen remarkable things today."

LUKE 5:17-26

SECOND
CHANCES

A NEW LIFE

Daniel Goldberg was having a rough go at life. Really rough.

He looked like a man who had never experienced a problem. At least, not one he couldn't conquer. But that was only the exterior.

Despite being an award-winning commercial real estate banker, Daniel's ambition and drive never seemed to answer those deep interior questions of "Who am I?" and "Where am I going?" He had fought drug addiction much of his life, and he lost his marriage in divorce all while trying to keep it together on the outside. He lived for worldly success and recognition—which he earned—but things were not working for him. Daniel's life was coming apart at the seams. He was a shell of a man. Raised a Jew but calling himself an atheist, Dan knew that he was a lost soul, one who really needed a miracle—if miracles even existed...

That miracle arrived through *The Passion of the Christ.*

CHANGED LIVES

Dan and his fiancée, Marsha Witt, were interviewed for the TV special "Changed Lives: Miracles of the Passion" at his home in West Palm Beach, Florida. There they gave us a very personal behind-the-scenes story of how that miracle happened.

Miracles of the Passion (M.O.T.P.)

Tell us about the Dan Goldberg we might have met two years ago.

With a shake of his head and a wry smile that tells a story in itself, Dan leaned back in the thick sofa with Marsha seated next to him, and began his tale.

Dan Goldberg

Dan Goldberg was a very lost soul two years ago, someone who had just gotten divorced and was trying to regain his identity. Right after the dissolution of my marriage, I spent a lot of time just trying to figure things out. I was very confused. I began to write as much as I could on paper, trying to find myself.

I thought I was being a very spiritual person, but I think I was merely philosophizing my own thoughts on what had gone wrong in my life. I didn't know who I was. I was just kind of lost.

M.O.T.P.

How were you lost?

Dan

I had no foundation of faith. When I was a young kid, I was an atheist. My family was…we were Jewish, but we were very reformed. We really didn't have any structured beliefs. Holidays were merely getting together with family; we would have eaten bacon on Hanukkah!

Throughout my teenage years, I was a drug addict. I did horrible things to my body.

As Dan continues, he shows us some photos of himself growing up. There we see a teenage boy, like anybody's kid, with long hair and wide smiles; one great disguise that probably had a lot of people fooled as to the pain that was going on inside.

M.O.T.P.

How did you navigate through that period of your life?

Dan

I knew what I had to do to get through each day. I did drugs. That helped. I went to school, came home, and did some more drugs. I went through drug rehabilitation centers. Two of them. It wasn't easy.

Sometimes I ask myself that same question: "How did I get here?"

M.O.T.P.

What was the beginning of the process that brought you to the place you are in today?

Dan

I think a lot of it had to do with meeting Marsha.

Marsha, a pretty woman with eyes that light up the room, nuzzles against Dan's shoulder. There's no question that these two are in love. But the man she's in love with today is very different from the man she met two years ago.

Marsha Witt

We worked at the same bank; we were friends. Dan was so much fun to be around; he made work a different experience. When the bank we worked at together was closed down, we still kept in touch. When we met up again at a friend's barbeque, he asked me out for dinner, coffee, and then the relationship grew from there. It was like an instant connection, instant friends.

Dan

The way she was living her life was so attractive to me. It was something I didn't have. Marsha was brought up in a great home, and she is a wonderfully spiritual person. She has this free spirit-type of personality, and inside I felt so trapped. There was a dimension of what she had that I was so intrigued by and so wanted to be a part of. I just needed to learn more about it. I'm so grateful I did.

M.O.T.P.

How did you learn more?

Dan

Just by going to church, being around her, knowing what kind of background she had, being around such wonderful unconditional love. Just such a closeness and forgiveness of people. And I thought, *Man, this is totally for me.* Surrounding myself with her and her faith helped me to understand some of the things that happened in my life and why I was able to get through them.

Being with Marsha made me want answers to the questions I had. I wanted more; I wanted to understand what this spiritual thing was. You see, I had no idea.

It's said that "opposites attract...but they usually don't stay together very long." Would Marsha want to stay with a man who at heart was a lost soul? Could Dan truly embrace a relationship with a woman who was so very different from him—someone who truly knew who she was when he didn't know who he was?

The answer would grow from an experience with a God Dan didn't even believe in, but soon would meet, up close and personal.

Dan

When *The Passion of the Christ* came out, Marsha's church, where she now works, went to see it. The pastor actually rented the entire movie theater so that all of the staff in the church could view it in the morning. Unfortunately, I was working, so I couldn't go see it.

M.O.T.P.

So, Marsha, you had the chance to see the movie first without Dan. What was it like for you?

Marsha's usually bright, expressive face turned solemn as she recalled the experience.

Marsha

I have always read in the Bible how the Lord died, but I was not prepared for what I saw on the screen. In the Bible it says about the crucifixion that Jesus was bloodied and disfigured. However,

until I saw it as it was on the screen, my mind had never fully grasped it.

After seeing *The Passion*, I was broken… so broken inside. I wanted to find the joy in Jesus' death because He died for me. Yet watching His death portrayed in the theater, all I could think about was how horrible it was. It was really, really hard for me.

Later I said to Dan, "You know, you're going to have to prepare yourself for what you are going to see."

Wanting to go to the film, Dan wasted no time and went to a screening the following night. There is no way he could have known what was waiting for him.

Dan

The movie affected me beyond comprehension. Here I was, this guy who came from being an atheist, being a drug addict, being unstructured, not being able to say the word "Jesus Christ" two years ago, being somebody who was so incredibly lost, sitting in a movie theater and finding Jesus Christ.

All my life I've treated myself horribly and treated other people horribly. I took drugs, skipped school, and refused to believe that there even was a God.

And then, there on the screen, before my eyes is this Jesus Christ, being beaten beyond recognition and yet having the love in His heart to forgive those who were crucifying Him by saying, "Forgive them; they know not what they do."

I cried like a baby.

Behind his glasses Dan's eyes were clear and resolute. He leaned forward as he recalled the turning point for him in the film.

Dan

Then came the part in the movie where Jesus' mom was remembering a moment when Jesus was a little boy. As a child,

He had fallen down and she ran to pick him up. Now, as Jesus carries the cross, He falls again. She runs to Him and kneels beside him.

Jesus puts His hand on her face and speaks. "I make all things new."

That's what it was for me. Jesus was making all things new for me.

Here was a man who was lost, without identity, without purpose, a failure in marriage, a failure in so much of life, living only for the accolades of other bankers. And here was God speaking directly to him in that theater, saying, "Dan—I can make *you* a new life! I make all things new!"

Dan Goldberg's miracle had begun.

Dan

I wanted to learn a lot more about Jesus. I became very reflective over my own life. I mean, this man was all-encompassing love and forgiveness.

Marsha and I had gone into a bookstore; we were just chatting. I think we were talking about the movie because we had been talking about it for days. We turned down an aisle in the bookstore and suddenly stopped talking. Right in front of us were Bibles.

And for me, that was just like, "Okay. I hear You."

They were "coincidentally" standing in the middle of the Bible section of the store! They were surrounded by God's Word. Dan laughed, recognizing God has the ultimate sense of humor.

Dan

I started digging through the Bibles to find the perfect one for me. I said, "I've got to get one that was completely layman, that would speak to me, you know, the Bible for dummies."

Dan

I was compelled one night to go to Marsha's house and shut the door, to be accepted by Christ and accept Him into my life. That moment was an incredible experience. Just incredible.

M.O.T.P.

Can you describe it for us?

Dan

My entire life started flashing before me. I felt as though everything I had ever done was running through me. For me to think of so many things and to be forgiven…it was the most incredible release and renewal because I was able to be forgiven for all of the horrible things that I have done, those things that I thought I never could be worthy of being forgiven for…for so much. My heart just poured out my eyes.

I was set free.

Daniel Goldberg, born and raised in a Jewish home, has seen a movie about the Jewish Messiah—a film that some had predicted would be anti-Semitic. Yet Dan's reaction was quite the opposite: He accepted Jesus Christ as the Messiah He claimed to be.

Mitch Glaser, a Messianic Jew (a Jew who believes Jesus is the Messiah) is with Chosen People Ministries in New York City. He has some very personal insights as to what Dan was experiencing, and the personal cost it might involve.

Mitch Glaser

It's a very big deal for a Jewish person to accept Jesus as their Messiah. As Jews, we learn at our mother's knee that Jews do not believe in Jesus. We are taught from a young age that when a Jewish person becomes a believer in Jesus, they are no longer a Jew. That's because Jewish people believe Christians become Christians the same way that Jews become Jews—you become a Christian by being born that way.

Any Jew who becomes a believer in Jesus should expect to be somewhat ostracized from the Jewish community because you've crossed a line, so to speak. It's almost like committing ethnic suicide; you've crossed a line and moved yourself out of the community.

Dan and Marsha are no longer opposites that initially attracted. Their hearts are now closely linked together through their common belief in Jesus—the center of their lives. Walking together arm-in-arm on the beach, Dan's smile has not vanished.

M.O.T.P.

Dan, some people who don't necessarily share your point of view might say that what you're experiencing is just temporary, something that is going to pass—a phase. What would you say to them? What would you say to your family?

Dan

For those people who think that this is just a phase, I think I'd probably chuckle because that was what I would have said once. "It's just a phase. He's going through a 'Jesus phase.' He just saw the movie." You know, that's cool if they think that. I know who I am. This is not just a phase; it's the rest of my life.

He knows who he is. Something he could never say before today.

Dan

As I mentioned, my family is Jewish, very reformed. I am trying to figure out the right time to tell them. Because even though I am not ashamed of what I am doing, my family is my family, and it's hard to be judged by those you love. I am hoping that they will accept me for who I am and who I am becoming.

M.O.T.P.

What do you think of who Dan is becoming, Marsha? How is Daniel different from the Daniel you knew before *The Passion*?

Marsha

Gosh, it's so evident to me that he is living life with a purpose higher than his own. Before he was living for material things, how much money he could make or what kind of job he could get. When he goes to work now, Dan isn't working for himself or anyone else around him. He knows he is working for God.

M.O.T.P.

What does that look like?

Marsha

Well, when he has a bad day, he handles it differently. He doesn't become angry, and he doesn't hold on to it. He lets it go, saying, "You know what? Today was a good day because I'm alive and I have a higher purpose now in life."

M.O.T.P.

How has going to *The Passion* changed your own walk with God?

Marsha

My love for God has just taken off. I always loved Him, but now when I read a verse in the Bible I understand it. The night after I saw *The Passion,* I read Romans 8:38-39: "I am persuaded that nei-ther death nor life, nor angels nor principalities nor powers, nor things present nor things to come, nor height nor depth, nor any other created thing, shall be able to separate us from the love of God which is in Christ Jesus our Lord" (NKJV).

Before *The Passion* it hadn't occurred to me I can't be sepa-rated from the love of God because of what Christ did. I see now how He became separated from God on my behalf. He did that so I would never have to be apart from God.

I love Christ for what He has done. Before I loved Him because I knew what He did. Now I love Him because I truly understand what He did. He took on the pain I will never have to take on.

M.O.T.P.

Marsha, tell us. Were you in love with Dan before all this hap-pened?

Marsha

I was! I was attracted to his humor. And he has a gentle heart, so wanting to give. However, I always thought I would fall in love with somebody who was on the same spiritual level as myself. I didn't understand why I had such a connection with this person or why I loved him so much.

Now I do. God knew that one day Dan would accept Him and that we would have this awesome spiritual relationship.

For me, it's like all of my dreams are coming true.

M.O.T.P.

How about your relationship now? How has sharing this movie experience changed the dynamic between you and him?

Marsha

Well, when we say hurtful things to each other—which hap-pens, we get into arguments and say things—we think about the images we saw in the movie and they help us see what we are fighting over. I'll say, "You know, remember that part in the movie?" And, he'll say, "Yeah."

We just have a different understanding between us now. Here's an example. When I bought a hardcover book of *The Passion* with pictures taken throughout the production, I was standing in the middle of Barnes and Noble and reading with tears running down my face. There's Dan's fiancée crying in the middle of the store and, you know, he wasn't ashamed at all. He understood.

M.O.T.P.

It sounds as though you two have connected on a deeper level than before.

Marsha

You could say we have spiritual intimacy now.

M.O.T.P.

To someone who might not share your faith or understand what you are talking about, what do you mean by spiritual intimacy?

Marsha

I had always heard about couples talking about this intimacy, how they would have devotions together. If they were having a bad day, they could call each other and say, "Please pray for me."

Before *The Passion,* Dan and I didn't have that together. Now we do. Whenever we're upset about something or upset with each other, we take it to God and release it. We look at each other with the love of Christ and not with the love of the world. And that's awesome. It's a very amazing feeling.

Our relationship has gone to a higher level.

M.O.T.P.

Some people might say this is just a phenomenon; that its just a fad. You know, everybody's getting on this Jesus bandwagon because of this movie. It'll pass.

Marsha

It's not a fad, and it's not just a mountaintop experience. Dan feels it, he knows it, and he accepts it. What I see about Danny is that he smiles a lot more. He has peace in his life, a peace I did not see in his life before.

Dan

The biggest part for me is the love factor. How I love people—I love people through Jesus. He loves through me. I feel as though I'm accepting a lot more of people because He has accepted me for who I am. Who am I to judge people anyway?

I'm not perfect by any means. I know that I'm going to mess up a hundred times. Yet, in everything that I'm do now I take God into consideration. The love that I have going into this marriage with Marsha is not the love that I had going into my first marriage. Then, it was not the love of Christ. It was me trying to love.

In a nutshell, I am a free man. I am free to love. I am free to be good-hearted.

I can sleep at night.

For Dan Goldberg, that is a miracle. He is a new man. He knows who he is. He has a new life.

It has been nearly three weeks since I saw the rough cut of The Passion. *It is still impacting my life. I can't stop thinking about it, nor can I stop talking about it. I have never seen a film that has so affected my life.*
—DEL TACKETT, EXECUTIVE VICE PRESIDENT, FOCUS ON THE FAMILY

CHANGED LIVES

I was saved in 1989, but I never really knew the Christian life as I should. My life wasn't transformed. I didn't feel power or see prayers answered. And so in anger and frustration, I decided to ignore God since He was ignoring me. And I thought I was happy living that way. I've suffered from depression for as long as I can remember. Of course, it didn't get better. It only got worse. And I also began to have a crisis at work.

There were other, smaller things going on also, and they all added up to bring me to the lowest of low points. In my free time I was planning what would be the best and fastest way to kill myself, and, most importantly, how to do it without being detected. If I was going to do it, I wanted it done right and permanently. I didn't want anyone to find me at the last moment and save me.

That's the state of mind I was in when I went to see *The Passion of the Christ* the second weekend it was out. I was—and I don't think I'm overstating it—traumatized by what I saw. I was so sick and stunned when we left the theater that I wasn't able to drive. My husband had to drive my car to our house. I didn't sleep but a couple of hours that night. I stayed awake reading my Bible.

It really hit me in the movie that Christ chose to die that horrid death for me. And I had been throwing it back in His face, saying it wasn't good enough. Reading about it was like reading a fairy tale; it stays very abstract. Seeing it happen like that made it real, so very real. I had no idea what the depth of His suffering might have been like.

So many movies show a token flagellation, and the Bible describes it in a handful of sentences. This movie made it live, made it real, made me face Christ's sacrifice and deal with it and the implications. I'll never be the same person after this. I can't earn what He did or be good enough, but I want to live now in a way that shows that I am grateful for it, so grateful.

Yes, now life is worth living. It's sweeter and precious now that I truly know my Lord.

—Internet submission

Watching the movie was very tough, and there were many times that I had to close my eyes while my body shook in hearing the pain inflicted on Him. He endured it all for me, and the movie brought Jesus' sacrifice to life. Now it's time for me to shake off my struggles and press on for everything that God has planned in my life.

Tanya—San Antonio, Texas

The Passion of the Christ is a movie that has changed my life. It filled me once again with the Spirit, something that I need so deeply…

—Carmel Valley, California

I have a daughter in Dallas who called and asked questions for two hours last night. Also another daughter who called and talked for over an hour. A niece called this morning asking questions, and we talked way over an hour. This film is causing people to get back into the Word, which is really exciting to me. I'm 73 years old and I, too, have a desire to read the Gospels—beginning with John.

—Mary Lou, Brown City, Michigan

Christianity is a religion that demands a response. It's not a religion that says, now here's some information, now go live a nice way. It is a faith system that requires us to respond and so this film helps us understand what it is and who it is we are responding to. What is it that Jesus wants from us if he went through what the motion picture said he did?

—LEE STROBEL, BESTSELLING AUTHOR
OF *THE CASE FOR CHRIST*

Whatever we do, it is because Christ's love controls us. Since we believe that Christ died for everyone, we also believe that we have all died to the old life we used to live. He died for everyone so that those who receive his new life will no longer live to please themselves. Instead, they will live to please Christ, who died and was raised for them.

So we have stopped evaluating others by what the world thinks about them. Once I mistakenly thought of Christ that way, as though he were merely a human being. How differently I think about him now! What this means is that those who become Christians become new persons. They are not the same anymore, for the old life is gone. A new life has begun!

2 CORINTHIANS 5:17-21 NLT

MIRACLES BEHIND THE SCENES

LIGHTNING BOY

Among the many incredible stories that took place during the actual filming of *The Passion of the Christ*, probably the best-known story is that of "Lightning Boy." His is a truly amazing account of God's miraculous hand of protection—and of faith renewed.

They say "lightning doesn't strike twice."

Well, not in this case.

CHANGED LIVES

Before *The Passion*, Italian-born Jan Michelini (pronounced Yan Mikka-leeny) would have described himself as a "mechanical Catholic"…a young man who went to mass because it was—as he would put it—a "familiar habit." For many years, Jan had asked God, "Show me the way. Let me understand. Give me a sign."

Jan worked as the key production assistant (PA) on the set of *The Passion*, doing various errands, helping with the details. It was a tremendous opportunity for him.

Little did he know that it would also be a tremendous show of God's power and presence.

Jan got the sign he'd been looking for.

Two signs in fact…

From Rome, Italy (in a strong, unmistakable Italian accent), Jan tells a story almost impossible to believe.

Jan Michelini

> I was struck by lightning twice; they call me "The Lightning Boy." I am also listed in the titles, the final titles at the end of the movie as Jan "Lightning Boy" Michelini. That's very funny...

 How often does a man struck by lighting live to tell about it—much less laugh about it?

There were many miracles occurring on the set of the film. One woman had a young daughter who had been having epileptic seizures— the little girl was miraculously healed. One of the actors portraying a sadistic Roman guard flogging Christ happened to be a Muslim. As he worked on the film he unexpectedly experienced the truth of who Jesus was—and is—and he became a Christian, a follower of Christ. Two other men on the film decided to leave their careers in the entertainment business to enter full-time ministry...serving God and serving others.

I assure you, this is *not* business as usual on a Hollywood film set! But this was not your usual Hollywood film either. As Mel Gibson was portraying the sacrificial death of God's Son, God made Himself present in the most unexpected ways.

It was during the filming of the crucifixion scenes when Jan had his first personal encounter from above. The crew was shooting in a picturesque town in the south of Italy when a nasty-looking storm blew in, threatening their production schedule.

Jan

I was struck the first time by lightning in Matera, a town in which we shot most of the crucifixion. I was on the "Golgotha ground" (the scene where the crosses were erected) and a storm was coming in.

It was starting to rain, so the stunt coordinator, Stephan Mioni, starts screaming in English, "Okay, guys. Everybody runs away now, because it's getting dangerous over here." You know, crosses and cranes everywhere.

Lightning rods.

As the key PA, part of Jan's responsibilities included coordinating actors and production crew going to and from the set. When Jan heard Stephan's orders to evacuate the set, he was near the production trailers, which were offices and facilities for the actors.

Jan

I was near the trailers with Luca Lionello [the actor who played Judas]. He told me, "No, stay here, stay here. It's not safe." And I say, "I have got to go back to check if someone is left on the set."

As Jan headed toward the set, rain began to beat down harder and harder. Carrying an umbrella, Jan saw just ahead of him an assistant director and a stuntman.

Jan was a walking lightning rod.

Jan

I was two meters from them when lightning struck my umbrella and I was shocked. My hand became big. It was just one second. The feeling is like a big contraction you have and your pressure goes up really high. I had some light burnings on my hand. I ran

into the trailers with all these people around me. And they say,
"What happened? What happened? We saw this lightning coming
down."

Approximately 30 percent of people struck by lightning die,
and 74 percent of lightning strike survivors have permanent
disabilities. To all those who had witnessed it, none of them
could believe that Jan had been struck by lightning right before
their eyes...yet there he was, standing before them...and, other
than a minor burn on his hand, he was perfectly fine!

As if that wasn't enough...

Jan

The funniest thing is that I took the lightning a second time.

Funny?

It was eight months later. The production crew was filming
some additional footage near Rome on a mountaintop called
Monte Guadagnolo.

Jan

We were shooting the Sermon on the Mount with Jim Caviezel.
There is a flashback in the movie about it. We were walking up to
the set, finally ready after hours of preparation of this scene—and
it was starting to rain.

Mel wanted to shoot something before the rain was getting
hard, so we were in a hurry. I was holding this umbrella and walking
with Jim Caviezel, holding his arm and stepping up on this mountain when a hairdresser, Teresa, started screaming, "Guys, hold the
umbrella! Otherwise my wig is going to get damaged."

So, I was arm-to-arm with Jim and I tell him, "Jim—we're gonna
be struck by lightning with an umbrella up here." And Jim acts like

I was joking with him. He says, "You are with *me*. Don't worry." I say, "All right."

Jim was joking, of course. He wasn't *really* Jesus, and he knew that he could not command the storm to stop as Jesus once did.

He got that part right.

Jan

We were up to the point of shooting, and two bolts came down. One took Jim, and the producer, Steve McEveety, saw lightning coming out of Jim's ears. And his hair was straight out. You can see it in the movie, in the flashback on the long shot, he has some hair this way.

Jim Caviezel later commented that it looked as though he had paid a visit to boxing promoter Don King's hairdresser!

Jan

The actors, 10 or 20 of them, fall down on the ground, scared. This was right before the action, and Jim decided to go on and act anyway…he wasn't hurt.

I ran to a car, and I didn't want to get out of it. My nose started bleeding.

Struck by lightning a *second* time—and all he had was a little nosebleed! People just don't walk away from being struck by lightning. They die. They are seriously burned or injured. Jan may have been unlucky—and maybe unwise to be holding an umbrella on a hilltop with lightning approaching—but he was not closed-minded. He knew something was up with him and God.

Jan

The funniest thing—I mean funny but weird at the same time—is that there were so many umbrellas opened. So, you say, "You choose me a second time? What do You mean? What do You want to tell me?"

It was like a miracle, you know. It's hard to speak about miracles, but it was *Someone* who protected us. I received many answers in my life from those two lightning strikes. I was going to change my life.

There were few who worked on the film who weren't touched in some way. Jan became close friends with two who were: Francesco De Vito, who played Jesus' disciple Peter, and Luca Lionello, who played Judas, His betrayer. Both men's characters betrayed Jesus in different ways, and both men knew that in their own lives, they had done so as well.

Francesco De Vito

This movie has changed my life very, very much. I can say completely. Now I can feel my aim. I searched myself and I went very, very deep inside of me. I asked myself many questions about my life. And now, I think that I have my answers.

My life has changed. I started to pray every day. Now I am aware of my passion, of my faith. I am aware what I would like to be. What I was, what I am…and what I want to be.

I understand the pain of Jesus. I understand His sacrifice. I understand why He was on the cross for us. That's why this movie is so important. I think for each one of us. For every human being.

Luca Lionello agrees. He is a man of few words who faced some important decisions at this time in his life, and he was unsure of which way to turn. But God showed up and brought light into a dark circumstance.

Luca Lionello

The path of my life has changed. I was at an intersection. And thanks to this experience, I have chosen the right path.

Jan

This movie changed our lives. We go with conviction to the Mass on Sunday. We understand now the sacrifice that Jesus Christ made for us and the meaning of the Eucharist [taking communion].

For a few months we had been living close to Jesus Christ's suffering for us. There are people who realize it and there are other ones who don't, but many of us who were on the set realized that we were living a very important moment in our lives.

It has given me a deep dialogue with God. I had to realize that I have a way…if God exists, then I have to believe in Him. And I have to walk with Him. I think there's a mission for everybody, each one of us on this earth. I'm going to see what happens.

I guess it's good that sometimes we don't have enough sense to come in out of the rain…otherwise we might not hear God's voice and receive those "signs" we too often ask for!

Not that I recommend intentionally putting yourself in harm's way to see how God might rescue you (in fact, I do *not* recommend this!)…but when you find yourself there, remember that He is there too…and a miracle is definitely waiting.

You can be a "lightning boy" or "lightning girl" too!

JIM CAVIEZEL

A lot of the focus in Hollywood is on the people who make the movies. If there's a star, people want to know all about him or her. Celebrities like Mel Gibson and Jim Caviezel—who portrayed Jesus in *The Passion of the Christ*—are human magnets to a lot of folks.

There's been an interesting paradigm shift in this movie. While Mel and Jim must certainly enjoy the celebrity that comes with creating a phenomenal film, it appears they would prefer the focus be elsewhere: on Jesus Himself.

CHANGED LIVES

Jim Caviezel was working on a film after he finished *The Passion,* and a buddy of mine was producing it. I really wanted to talk with Jim about his experiences and hear firsthand how he was a different man. I suspected he could speak to miracles and changed lives as well as anyone because he had had the unique experience of portraying the Redeemer of the world in the redemptive act of all time.

My friend arranged for us to meet on the stages where they were finishing up the music for the film. We met, discovered we had some mutual friends on the SEAL teams, had some lunch, and then went over and sat down to a 40-minute inter-view.

I liked Jim right away. He seemed very introspective and thoughtful—soft-spoken and careful with his words. We shared concerns about challenges in the church and how we need to take life as believers in Jesus a lot more seriously. It was evident he considered his job as an actor an honor and a responsibility. This would not be your typical "Hollywood star" interview.

One thing I discovered right away: His prayer was that people seeing the film would not see Jim, but that they would see Jesus.

That prayer was answered...big time.

After meeting with Mel Gibson and hearing that he was going to make a film authentic to the Christian faith, Jim knew *The Passion* was going to be a very powerful film but also that it would divide.

The film would upset people because it was presenting the truth about Jesus Christ. People sitting and watching the last 12 hours of Jesus' life would be faced with the decision of whether Jesus was God as He claimed...or was this man, bru-tally killed in His innocence, a liar and dying in vain? This is not your typical matinee fare. And with the controversy that was sure to follow such a film subject, Jim had a choice to make when Mel Gibson presented the role to him. With careful thought given to his life and faith, Jim realized he owed it to God to do this movie.

And when the process for the film began, Jim was certain that it transcended typical film...to the point that it can no longer just be considered a film. It is an experience that says to people, "I have got to get right, right now!" It is an encounter with Christ.

During our conversation, Jim and I discussed how men make time for what they want, what they feel is important. And the reason man does not make time for God is because he does not love God. At some point, this film poses hard questions to the audience: Do you really love Him? Do you call Him "the Way" but decide not to follow Him?

When Jim started the film, he was trying to get involved with the languages. His biggest challenge and what he felt would be his personal miracle was learning the complicated languages enough that he could speak from his heart.

He faced this obstacle with prayer. As a Roman Catholic he would begin with the Rosary. Then he would go to the Mass. He also spent significant time in the Scriptures. There were times he didn't want to pray or he lacked the energy, but it became an act of faith and discipline that would carry him through the grueling production.

While working on the film, Jim faced a truth we all face if we are honest with ourselves and with God...he did not love enough. God challenged him to love more. He felt humbled, knowing that the Holy Spirit asks us to work on our strengths—the talents God has given us—but also our weaknesses.

Many times Jim did not feel worthy of the task before him, but he had to dare to try. With great humility he understood the significance and importance of playing Christ because this presentation, this movie experience, could help people—help them see truth.

Back to prayer. Again and again he had to come back to praying because of whom he was playing. Christ had to be inside him…and the inspiration and strength of his perform-ance. This kind of praying drew him to what was a great mir-acle—an understanding that he didn't want people to see *him* on the screen. He only wanted the audience members to see Christ. And this became his daily prayer.

This is the miracle that transformed a performance into an experience.

No one can be passive about *The Passion*. Even if someone walked out or said they didn't believe any of it, there is nothing passive about the emotions it stirs and how it speaks to the heart of anyone who watches or has been involved in the filming. Those who resist seeing the film do so with a disclaimer that it isn't their "thing" or their "answer." But they just don't want to deal with a confrontation with truth.

People have responded in many ways to *The Passion*. Some have laughed at the idea of attending this movie. But there are others who are brave, see it, and believe. All of these people and their places along the faith journey are represented on that screen…those whose hearts are sold out for God, those who laugh at the idea of a Savior, and those who are brave enough to find answers to their deepest questions.

The day after Mel Gibson offered Jim the role, he then basi-cally tried to talk him out of it. When Jim asked Mel why he was trying to deter him, Mel explained that what Jim would have to do for this role, for this experience, would be extremely difficult. Jim responded with strength. He was willing to carry the cross or be crushed by it.

At this point in his conversation with Mel, Jim brought up the fact that his initials are J.C. and he was 33 years old. The same age as Christ on the cross.

This is just one of several "coincidences" and flat-out miracles on the set of the movie. Another one relevant to an actor's name is Maia Morgenstern, who played the Virgin Mary. "Morgenstern," means "Morningstar," who is called the "Blessed Mother." Such miracles appeared as signals of grace to many on the set, and they happened over and over again during the filming.

The now much-publicized account of Jim being struck by lightning is one of those more powerful "signals of grace." He was high up on a hill and just knew he was going to get hit. They were about to roll the camera and his hair started to stand up. Within seconds, he looked at others in front of him and their eyes lit up as though they were going to cry. Then, boom! Witnesses said they saw fire on the right and left sides of his head.

When Jim was hit, he should have been hurt. But he wasn't. From that moment, he felt that nothing was going to stop this film. This was a movie that even after being shown in theaters will continue to live.

Anyone who turned on their television during this time knows that *The Passion* happened amid attacks...verbal attacks against Mel Gibson, against the Christian faith, and against the representation of Christ as more than a "good person" or leader.

Thirteen years before *The Passion*, Jim felt led to be an actor, and at the time, he didn't know why. He recalls telling his dad, who responded that if God wanted him to be anything, it would be a priest. Yet God has been preparing Jim his whole life for this. And if he hadn't gone through these years of preparation, he would have never been ready for the question from Mel Gibson asking him to play Christ. Every ounce of his flesh wanted to yell no, but his heart was able to say yes.

And that response led to a time like no other in his life. He witnessed miracles big and small. Just making it through the process was a miracle in itself. Getting up at 2:00 A.M., going till 10:00 at night. Special-effects makeup itching like mad, having a dislocated shoulder, getting on a cross and experiencing hypothermia, which was horrendously painful. Then, in the midst of being freezing cold, on the cross he started to experience suffocation.

Most of the time, he couldn't eat or keep food down. He would throw up lunch all the time. His body couldn't digest anything because of the hypothermia. He had times when his whole body was shutting down.

At the end of the day, he would take a two-hour hot shower in which two people scrubbed him down to get off the makeup. Now, you would think being in a hot shower would be nice after being out in the cold, but what ends up happening is that the heat makes you want to throw up...which he did.

Three hours of sleep, then up again at 2:00 A.M. Repeat the same thing for five weeks.

Jim said he was miserable and at times didn't know how he could continue. So many times he wanted to quit but, for him, it was as when Peter said to the Lord, "Where will we go?" He had nowhere else to go. He knew he had to finish this thing.

It was truly a miracle he was able to pull that off. And through that miracle of endurance and perseverance, the miracle Jim had asked for happened…people watching the last 12 hours of Christ's life would not see Jim at all…they would see Christ. Only Christ.

Though Jim was aware of many good things that took place during the filming of *The Passion,* he was also aware of evil things that happened. But somehow—or rather because of Someone—everyone came through to create the most remarkable "religious" film ever made.

Even during the height of the controversy over the film, there was peace because Jim knew that if this were not a controversial film, then they had not done a very good job. What controversy is there if Christ is just a good person? What did He say about loving your neighbor? You know, if you love only those who love you, what good is that? No, love your enemy. Do good to those who hurt you. And as much as these messages should incite unity, they don't…not in the world. They are words that divide.

The relevance of this film for today is easy to see…just look around. There are the means and the will to destroy the world. We have witnessed this in the terror of September 11 and in the aftermath that has followed. This film can open a truth for those willing to hear and that could prevent some serious devastation on mankind.

People of faith surrounding or directly involved in the film knew it would be successful if it was done not how man would want it but how God needed it to be made—and that would be in a controversial way. It would be the complete opposite of the world, this world that knew Him not.

How does someone feel after playing Christ? How does someone look at their own life from that point on? It was very easy for Jim to get down on himself for falling short sometimes. But what kept him going is that original question from the Holy Spirit, "Can I love more?" And to this question he prays his heart will answer, "Yes. Yes, I can love more."

I've interviewed a lot of celebrities over the years and am friends with several. They're mostly regular folks like you and me. But Jim stood out in an unusual way. I really had to work at seeing him as Jesus. I was right there, face-to-face, but it was Jim Caviezel, not Jesus. (By contrast, Arnold Schwarzenegger *is* The Terminator, Jackie Chan *is* Jackie Chan…you can't get around it.)

But there came an unexpected moment. The interview was finished, and Jim and I were leaving the stage together. I had told him about the night-vision footage I'd shot of people's faces watching *The Passion of the Christ*. He was interested in that and curious as to the scenes people reacted to the most (the flogging scenes of course, I told him). As we finished talking, Jim asked about reactions to the scene in which Jesus carried and then embraced His cross—then he reenacted the action just as he had done in the film—hunching over, raising his arms over his shoulders as if he were carrying—and embracing—a cross.

I am emotionally moved as I write this.

All of a sudden Jim was not present—though physically he still was. It was as though I were standing directly beside Jesus carrying His cross to Calvary. He stood a foot away from me, looking into my eyes, embracing His cross, and asking me with His heart, His eyes, "How did they respond when I did this?"

"How did they respond when I did this?"
That is the single most important question of the film.

ALL FOR THIS

The "Changed Lives: Miracles of the Passion" documentary has been the most challenging project I've undertaken in 30 years in the entertainment biz. Every step along the way has been slippery, rocky, muddy, or a creaky wooden footbridge crossing a deep chasm. Thankfully, this has provided me with plenty of opportunities to trust *heavily* on God to carry me across to the other side. And whenever you do that, you're going to see miracles in your life.

I did.

CHANGED LIVES

While we were producing and editing the TV special, the days were long—18 hours, usually. Try that for a couple of months and see what kind of mood you'll be in. Add to that enormous financial uncertainties (I'd taken out a second mortgage on my home to fund the show, which had not been sold yet), and obligations I'd made to pay good wages to all my crew—producers, cameramen, editors—most of whom were personal friends (and thankfully still are), and the stress starts to add up quickly. I had some desperate prayer times that usually went something like this:

God, if You don't show up right now, I am sunk! It's over! I know You own the cattle on a thousand hills…well, I need You to sell one or two because I am about to be in deep trouble. I need You right now.

God loves that, I think.

A big problem with Christians in America is that we are not desperate for God, so we don't usually cry out to Him and expect Him—and *really* need Him—to show up right then. We're rarely in a situation where if God doesn't show up then we're going to die or lose our home or something else really bad will happen.

That happens a lot in places like Africa, Cambodia, and poor parts of South America, where needs are great and people are desperate for God. And guess what? He shows up! Just the way He promises. And what do you see in those places?

Miracles.

Miracles Because of Miracles

So I was desperate and, big-surprise, God showed up and supplied miracles. Financial provision over and over again, rest and refreshment beyond what a few hours sleep could provide, and terrific coworkers who believed in me but mostly in God. It was truly amazing to once again see God's hand very present in my time of great need. He was just waiting for me to learn to trust Him and see just how trustworthy He is.

And there was more. The project itself was taking on a life of its own, and miracles were happening. People who'd been praying for work and were near-destitute found employment. Talented entertainment professionals found answered prayer getting to work on a project that really mattered to them after working on mindless TV shows just to pay bills and be "creative" (if you're not in this business, you have no idea how morally debilitating this can all be). We developed wonderful, warm relationships with several of the people we interviewed for the show—and they so needed a Christian brother or sister right at that very moment.

As I said earlier, when God tells you to do something, it's a good idea to do it. From His perspective He can see the entire parade, from the beginning to the end. We only see that little part of the parade that is passing by us right then. We can't know when we might be part of a miracle.

That happened to me right in the middle of the whole process—at a time when I needed it.

We were getting some good press on the show, particularly after my appearance on *Good Morning America.*

Prior to one of the follow-up interviews with a national show, I was directed to a makeup room and introduced to Cindy, the makeup artist. She was going to make me look all nice (meaning tan and younger) for the live interview. We chatted for the 15 minutes while she performed her own miracle on me!

She was very interested in my show and about the miracles. I shared with her some of the incredible stories about how God had reached into these people's circumstances and rescued them, changing their lives forever. She shared that she used to go to church a long time ago but hadn't been in a while. It was clear she was hungry for some spiritual food, and she really wanted to know when my show was going to air so she could see it.

We finished, I went on the show, did my bit, said goodbye to the crew, and went downstairs to my waiting car, which was parked in front of the building.

"Coincidentally," Cindy was exiting the building at the same time, and because of the location of my car we walked together for a little bit. She had listened to my interview, heard the stories and seen a clip from my show, and reiterated how much she looked forward to seeing it.

I followed my heart's instinct and asked, "Out of curiosity, what part of town do you live in?"

She told me it was in the valley, and "coincidentally" not far from The Church On The Way, where I'm a member. Easter was in a few weeks, so I told her about the church, that we had a great pastor/teacher, that it's the "real deal," and that Easter is an excellent service and she ought to give it a try—I'd be there. It was kind of a lame invitation, but I didn't want her to think I was hitting on her…(which I wasn't, honestly).

She told me thanks and maybe she'd check it out. We said our goodbyes, "nice to meet you," and I got in my car and headed back to editing.

The long, laborious process of finishing the show continued for several more weeks, and on Easter weekend, the show finally aired.

On Easter morning the 11:00 service was packed, as usual. Close to 2000 people filled the large sanctuary. We had about five services that day to accommodate everyone, so close to 10,000 would celebrate Easter at The Church On The Way. I came early and got a good seat near the front. The music was triumphant, the lilies were magnificent. Christ was risen indeed! We took a moment to turn and greet people around us, and directly behind me sat a woman who looked familiar…it was Cindy! What were the odds of that?

I told her I was glad to see her there, "Happy Easter," and that was that.

The message was powerful and encouraging, and the entire service was moving.

I just love Easter.

At the end of the service, as is customary at our church, the pastor gives the opportunity for anyone who wants to start a new life with Christ to acknowledge that by raising their hand while everyone's head is bowed and they're given the courtesy of privacy. There are often a dozen or more people who make that life-changing decision in each service, and quite a few more on Easter. Then the pastor asks the person to gently tap the shoulder of the person beside them and tell them, "I'm inviting Jesus into my life."

Behind me, I heard Cindy whisper those words through her tears.

All those long days and short nights, all the trials and tribulations, all the fears and uncertainties, were suddenly all completely worth it.

If the only reason God had me create "Changed Lives: Miracles of the Passion" was so I would meet Cindy and invite her to church where she would start a new life with Him, then that was good enough for me. For Cindy, it's a miracle.

We only see a little part.

God sees the whole parade.

180-DEGREE TURNAROUND

The God-Hater

Sam Marte was an angry man. A drug dealer. Violent, powerful, and intimidating, Sam was the kind of guy who would not hesitate taking anything he wanted from anybody—and making them pay if they held out.

With a troubled childhood, he decided at the normally tender age of eight that there was no God.

He had a lot of reasons to be full of hate toward a God he claimed didn't even exist. How could there possibly be a loving God when so many bad things happened all around him? And now as a grown man, he was about to teach his young daughter that God is nothing more than a "silly fairy tale."

What Sam did not know was that a miracle was waiting for him in a movie theater.

CHANGED LIVES

Sam Marte

I used to call myself an atheist because it was politically correct. If you say you're a "God-hater," then "Whoa. I'm out of here. I don't want lightning to strike me." An atheist is, basically, a God-hater, 'cause they're against God. But "atheist" sounds decent. I can be around people and say "atheist" instead of "God-hater." And they'll either respect me or not respect me, but they'll listen to me more. Realistically, I guess I did believe in God because I blamed Him for most things.

Surprising words from a man who was raised in a Pentecostal church where his father was the minister. Attending church was a part of everyday life in Sam's family. Going to church sometimes four or five days a week and having his parents wrapped up in their ministry, Sam grew up knowing a lot about the Bible and all these "God" things.

But there's a big difference between knowing about God and actually knowing God.

Something big was missing for Sam. His parents were consumed with their work at the church and weren't as present with him as he needed as a young boy. He grew to resent the church, which was competing for his parents' affections. And by association, he grew to resent God.

The life he lived in the inner city of New York was rough. He didn't have the special places most American kids have where he could run and play, enjoy fresh air, and revel in God's creation. Young Sam Marte's world was dark, smelly, and filled with immorality—not a healthy place for a small boy to explore and try to discover what life is all about.

With each passing year, that claustrophobic environment made him more and more angry. Life didn't make sense to him. Then came a turning point that would direct him down an even darker, lonelier path that few return from.

Sam

I guess it started when I decided that I was no longer going to believe in God. I felt this way, maybe, when I was eight years old. Where I lived, my environment and what the Bible said didn't balance out.

I was brought up in the inner city. Not a nice neighborhood. No trees, no grass. I'd see pimps; I'd see prostitutes, drug dealers with nice cars, you know. So, I would guess there wasn't really a God. I'd see all these things happening and that He allowed it to happen. I decided there was no God.

I was going to the store, but I was supposed to go to church that night. I got hit by a car. That's where it all started, when I thought that God wasn't with me. I'm like, you know, there's not a God.

The downhill descent had begun.

By age 15, Sam was done doing his masquerade and going to church. He decided to draw a line in the sand. One Sunday morning, he went toe-to-toe with his father. What happened next almost landed Sam on the streets.

Sam

My father, as usual, got up and said to me, "Time to get dressed and praise the Lord." It was the last time I wanted to hear those words, so that Sunday I confronted him. Now, he's old-school. It's not like today, like we're talking now. "Okay, son. Let's talk about this." Then, it was "There's nothing to talk about. You're going to church whether you like it or not. You live in my house and you'll do as I say. You're going to church."

"I am not going to church." To say that, it's a big thing. I had never spoken to my father like that, ever. I told him, "If you force me to go to church, I will embarrass you." With him being the minister, how's he going to lead the people then? The Bible says you have to have your home in order. So, I used that. I used Scriptures to shake him up.

He thought about it and then told me I would be going to church or I could leave the house. I said, "Fine. This is your home. You throw me out, and I'll let the whole world see your leadership."

At 15 I was going to do as I pleased. I was not going to church because it's a way of keeping people, weak people, believing in something. Controlling them. That's what I thought. I was not going to be controlled by people saying I was going to hell. I refused to be a part of that group.

Sam had made his choice: God was out. Officially. And it didn't take long before his choice began radically affecting the way his life looked. He started making a name for himself on the streets; Sam was no longer that "church boy" others could mess with. He had a new family—one that helped him deal drugs, pick fights, beat up people, and rob stores. With his new associates, Sam got wanted he wanted: the reputation of someone you had better fear.

Sam

By the time I left the church, I felt that since God wasn't helping me, I was going to help myself. My idea was to leave church and become a big, tough guy. My friends were murderers, drug dealers, very tough guys. I was associated with them, and I didn't see anything wrong with that because they were my family at the time. They were the ones who were supporting me in my decision not to go to church, not to believe in God.

We were looking for a quick buck, and the only way to get a quick buck in my environment was to sell drugs, steal, or murder for money. Those were the options.

"Where's God now?" I would ask when someone got hurt. You know, to me it was confirmation. There wasn't a God. I used to have a 40-ounce Old English before going to school instead of a

glass of orange juice, and I thought that would bring about my tough-
ness.

See, when I was in church, I was getting picked on, getting beat
up. They knew I was a church boy and it was easy to pick on me.
They knew I wouldn't retaliate because it's not what I'm suppose
to do. I used to go home and tell my parents about getting beat
up. They'd tell me to look at what happened to Jesus. He was crucified but turned the other cheek. So, I got beat up for quite some
time.

Until I hit the streets. Then people started fearing me because
I had no fear in God. What I did to them and how it was demon-
strated in my character was "Before you mess with me, you'd better
know I'm not on God's side. I'm on the other side now. You will
get hurt."

And people did get hurt.

If there were students in his school Sam didn't like, he'd
threaten them and never see them back at that school again.
To show his contempt for anything related to God, Sam would
roll joints of pot with pages from a Bible and literally throw
the Bible across the room in disrespect.

One of Sam's buddies called Sam a hypocrite for carrying
money in his pocket because it said "In God We Trust" on it.
So Sam stopped carrying money on him—he would only carry
credit cards!

Sam Marte was one messed up guy. What few "friends" he
had were dope dealers and murderers—violent, hate-filled men
like himself. Life didn't look as though it were going to last too
long for a street thug like Sam.

He told himself he was fine with this. But he didn't have
much to live for. Depression and suicide were his constant com-
panions.

Sam

After I lost my faith, I had no one to turn to. Two of my friends had already committed suicide at the time. One of them had told us what he was going to do, but no one took him seriously. I was going through major depression at that time; I went to three different funerals in a week. I said, "You know, I'm ready to get out of here."

But inside I was saying, "This is another thing God's not going to control. I'll make my own destiny, and if I go to hell I'm going to curse God from hell."

My grandmother was the reason I didn't [kill myself]. She was a woman of God; she was a part of my life. I didn't want her to suffer. She meant more to me than anything.

One day she caught me smoking pot on a corner in her neighborhood with five or six friends. She had come over to tell us that that smoking pot was something that we shouldn't be doing. She didn't realize that it was me standing there...her own grandson with a joint in his hand. The other guys laughed; they see a big tough guy's grandma coming and they want to see how he's going to respond to that.

She just said, "You need to come with me." On the walk home, my grandmother wasn't judgmental. She said that what I was doing wasn't good for me, that I was going to destroy my life if I kept on.

She didn't bring God into it; she didn't say anything about Him because she knew I wouldn't listen if she did. She had seen who I was associating with and the potential they had as professional criminals and thugs, drug dealers and murderers.

As Sam grew older, he fell into a very tumultuous relationship with a woman, whom he married and would have two daughters with. This was a big deal, so he decided it was maybe time to make a few changes. External ones.

Sam

I knew that living the lifestyle I had been living was either going to put me in prison or get me killed. So I started working at a Fortune 500 company and turned my life around. I wanted to prove to my family that I could be a decent person and not believe in God.

I wanted to get married. I wanted a family. I wanted the American dream.

As his marriage got rough, Sam's contempt for God became stronger. He called himself an atheist, but he looked like a man playing chess with God—always trying to force Him into checkmate. When his daughter, Samantha, was about to be born, he was frighteningly and selfishly—and even bizarrely—adamant about keeping God far away.

Sam

When I had my firstborn, my wife's father, a minister, wanted to pray that she'd be born healthy. I wouldn't allow that to happen. I believed that prayer was begging God, and I was not going to do that. People around me would say, "What if your baby is born retarded or blind?" I had an answer to that too. I said, "I'm going to leave it in the hospital."

That was my answer. God was not going to win. It was me against Him, and I'd show Him.

The depression and thoughts of suicide from his younger years had never left Sam. Zoloft and eight drinks a day of hard alcohol were his coping mechanisms. He was a father, but with no real purpose to life and so much hatred in his heart—self-hatred—he had little reason for living.

He never actually tried suicide, but he intentionally lived very dangerously, hoping some tough guy would kill him, and his girls could get life insurance money. He'd pick fights with guys much tougher and meaner, hoping to get knifed or shot. It never happened. He once humiliated and threatened a Mafioso right in front of his associates—on purpose—sure that they'd do him in. They thought he was nuts and let him go.

If it wasn't so sad, it'd be a great scene from a movie. And there was more.

Sam

I was on the train with my two daughters, and there was this thug who was bothering people, a real intimidating person. He was picking on some young lady. I said to myself, *I'm going to show him the right thing. And then again, maybe this guy has a gun. He could shoot me.*

At least my kids would witness their father trying to help. So, I pulled him down and kicked him off the train. The guy just fell; I guess he felt intimidated because he's probably been doing this for years. The lady thanked me, but I was so [ticked] off. I was like, *That wasn't my goal. I was trying to help, but that wasn't really my goal.* I thought this guy was so tough that maybe he'd pull out a knife or gun and say, "Mind your own business." It happens all the time. My daughters would witness my death, collect insurance, and label me as a great man. A person who doesn't believe in God.

It wasn't obvious to Sam, but God believed in him. Sam's miracle was about to begin.

It was Ash Wednesday when *The Passion of the Christ* hit theaters in New York. Sam caught news reports covering the event and scoffed at the scenes of moviegoers coming out of the theater with stunned faces and tears, saying how impacting the film was. Then, drinking with friends at a bar, one of them said, "Let's go see *The Passion.*"

Sam

When *The Passion of the Christ* first came out, I turned on the news and saw people coming out of the movie, crying and saying it's a powerful movie. It's this and that. I'm like, "These people are so weak. You know, come on. These are actors."

To my friend I said, "All right." We went and I couldn't say "give me two tickets for *The Passion of the Christ.*" I couldn't come out and say that because I felt that maybe there's some sort of belief in me. So I cursed. I said, "Let me get two tickets for the blank, blank...."—I actually cursed Jesus instead of saying, "Let me get two tickets for *The Passion of the Christ.*"

That was my goal, to offend. Everybody in line looked at me. This...I don't know...atheist is coming to see the movie, huh? I was like, "You guys need to wake up. There's no Jesus, okay. It's a story...like Shakespeare." It was a fictional character. I thought it was a fiction character. This is not real.

I didn't go see the movie because I wanted my life to change. I went to see the movie to criticize it...to have another conversation piece with my friends and tell them how much I enjoyed the beatings because they weren't real to me. Jesus got stoned, got spit on, and I'm grinning. I'm looking around at the theater and everyone's crying. I'm like, "Wow, these people are so weak. This was a fairy tale. People, you need to wake up. This is a bunch of actors getting together, you know, and making a movie."

Just before Sam went into the movie, his cell phone rang. It was his nine-year-old daughter, Samantha, calling with a surprising request for her daddy. She wanted Sam to take her to see *The Passion of the Christ*.

Coincidence?

Samantha

I wanted to see the movie with my dad because he always takes me places. He's a good dad, and I just wanted to see it with him.

Sam

Standing there in the theater, I told Samantha that I had heard that the film was a little violent and rated R. I said, "I'm in the theater now, actually, and I'm going to screen the movie. If I think it's appropriate for you to watch it, I'll take you this weekend."

Now, I never break a promise with my daughter, so she was very happy.

After the movie let out, it wasn't long before Sam heard his cell phone ring again; it was Samantha asking what he thought about the movie. Agreeing to take her to see *The Passion* on Sunday, Sam made the decision that the time had come for Samantha to know about where he stood when it came to God.

Sam

My daughter wasn't aware that I was a radical atheist. I thought she was mature enough to know my views at that point. I was going to explain to my daughter that it's fiction and she's going to believe me that it's a fairy tale.

Sunday arrived and Sam kept his word to Samantha. He expected to feel nothing different from the first time he had seen the film just four days before. However, from the minute father and daughter walked into the theater, something was going on.

Sam had no idea, but God was very present with him and Samantha right there in the lobby.

Sam

I asked Samantha if she would like some popcorn. She didn't want any. She enjoys popcorn and soda, but for some reason she was very into the movie. She just said, "No, Dad. Just sit here."

Samantha

It wasn't really a popcorn movie. I knew it was a serious movie. Everybody was talking about it, and almost the whole world was seeing it

As the movie was about to start, Sam kept rehearsing in his mind what he would say to his daughter after the film was over.

Sam

That's the mentality I went in with the second time. I was going to explain to my daughter that this is fiction and she's going to believe me.

God knew Sam's motives too.

God cared for little Samantha—and He cared for Sam. All those years when Sam could have been killed by thugs or Mafioso or bad drugs…God loved him then and was watching over him…protecting him…for this moment.

The miracle.

Sam

I sat down and something came over me. I was looking at everything as if...as if I were there. I felt every word, every movement of the movie. It was incredible. In the back of my head I was like, oh, wait a minute. This is a movie, and I kept saying to myself, *Sam, this is a movie.* Wait, what's happening. I'm feeling—I'm getting some emotional feelings.

And I kept repeating to myself, *Nothing but a movie. They're actors. This is a story. I've been doing good without God; I'm healthy, have a job, my daughters are healthy.*

Sam's chess game continued...

Sam

I'm fighting with these thoughts back and forth. What if I'm wrong? What if I'm going to lead my daughter to the wrong path?

The movie ended and the two left the theater. Sam was very conflicted, unsettled, and confused. Very unlike his usual exterior.

Sam

When I left the theater, I was still a nonbeliever. I was like, it's a movie, yeah...and I'm not going to feel this way. But I was still having these feelings. I said to myself, *Let me get my thoughts together before I discuss my views and my beliefs with her because once I do, it's going to be forever.* So I told Samantha, "Honey, you're going to have to go home."

I was touched by the movie, but it had been so many years…You just don't turn around and be like—Okay, I've seen the movie and I believe in God. It's not that easy…not the way it works.

Or is it?

Even after taking Samantha home and buying a bottle of liquor, the feelings and thoughts Sam was having just wouldn't go away.

Sam

I still felt something in me that kept saying, "You know you're wrong. Be man enough to admit you're wrong."

Then my daughter called wanting to talk about the movie. I said, "We'll discuss it when I see you next time."

I was drinking my bottle of Hennessy, getting alcohol in the system. I was trying to do that purposely so that the thoughts would leave. And they did. I was drinking and playing my loud music and everything's cool. Sam, you're back. Yeah, I'm back. Went to sleep, got up that morning, and I couldn't fight the feeling. Part of my being was humbled. "I'm wrong," I said. "I don't know what's going on." I didn't know who to talk to. I couldn't call my parents to have them say, "It's God. It's Jesus and He's touched you."

I didn't want to hear that, you know. So I turned on my computer and typed in "Jesus Christ."

On his computer Sam found a website where there was a small prayer and a paragraph for those who wanted to accept Jesus Christ as their personal Savior. Sam got on his knees and prayed.

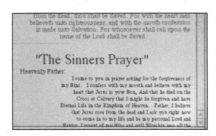

The miracle found its target.

Sam

You know, I made a decision. A decision to accept Jesus as my personal Savior humbled me. Once I read the prayer on the computer, I realized what I had done, that I had accepted Jesus Christ. I felt such peace.

I went to work. While riding the subway I kept thinking, *I feel different. I'm a believer now, and I'm okay.*

One of the first people who heard the news about what Sam had done was Anjanette Adams, one of his coworkers and a close friend.

Anjanette Adams

I had known Sam for about three years. Through the whole time I've known him, he's always been very respectful to me, a very nice person, but we had different views when it came to religion.

When Sam told Anjanette about the transformation that had just taken place in his life, she was surprised, happy, and a little doubtful all at once. But as days turned into weeks, she knew Sam had become a different man, from the inside out.

Anjanette

All the time I've known Sam I've never seen him cry. Since he's seen *The Passion,* he would start talking to me about "I don't see how people can't accept Jesus. Look at what He did for us." And he would well up with tears and walk out of my office. And I would say, "Sam! Come back!" You know, just like a husband...you get into an argument and he walks away. He would just walk away and I would be like, "Wow."

Sam

Some of my former friends, my old friends I used to hang out with, they basically laugh at me now. Some of them are, "This is gonna fade away. I'm giving you a week, a month, a year. It's gonna fade away, and you'll come back to your old sad self."

Another of Sam's friends believes the new Sam is here to stay. Manuel Gomez has known Sam for 18 years and is the godfather of his two daughters.

Manny Gomez

Our friendship has been like brothers—opposites but brothers. My views have been of Christian views, faith. Sam, on the other hand, has been an atheist. He did not believe in God and was very skeptical. For 18 years he's never even considered God or that there might be a supreme being. It's been a 180-degree turnaround from the Samuel I knew before *The Passion*. And it shocked me. I was flabbergasted because here's a guy who never discussed Jesus; he refused to. Now all of a sudden he's talking about God. Like I said, he's made a 180-degree turnaround.

When Sam called to tell me, I said, "You know, Sam, I hear the difference in your voice. I hear peace."

That inner peace has been the lasting miracle given to Sam through *The Passion of the Christ*.

Sam

I had a lot of questions about the Bible, and when I saw *The Passion of the Christ*, 85 percent of the questions were answered. That's the miracle.

Now, it's not like I believe in God and all of a sudden my problems disappeared. I'm still in the same place. I didn't hit the lotto.

Nothing has changed financially. I'm still divorced and still working the same job, nine to five.

The problems are the same problems; the change is now how I look at them. My outlook is different. Now I don't have God to blame. He's no longer my scapegoat. I'm taking responsibility when something happens now. I'm no longer smoking. No more Zoloft. When I get depressed, I go to the Bible.

So, what's the miracle? Peace. I am at peace. That's the miracle. I could die tomorrow and be very happy with my life. It just doesn't get much better than that.

THE TWO JEFFS

Iraq. Spring 2004.

American troops are on daily patrols throughout the embattled nation. Two soldiers who are close friends—both coincidentally named Jeff—serve in the same unit. Each day these two buddies set out from their fortified compound, unsure as to whether either will return alive. It is a stressful and unpredictable ever-changing environment.

The Passion of the Christ had just been released in the U.S., and, amazingly, pirated DVDs quickly appeared on the streets of Baghdad. One of these made its way to the unit of these young men. Several soldiers decided to watch it one night. After hearing all the press about it, they couldn't wait.

As expected, it was a very moving experience for all of them. Many of the men already had a relationship with God, but some did not. Only one of the Jeffs did.

Something that had been brewing inside the non-Christian Jeff came to the surface that night. For many weeks he'd seen death and tragedy up close and personal, and he'd also seen how his close pal, the other Jeff—a believer in Jesus—dealt with life's circumstances from a different perspective. The two Jeffs talked about the truth of Jesus' passion for every person, and how God was with them, right there in a war zone far from home in Iraq.

That night, the two friends and warriors became brothers as the nonbelieving Jeff made the decision to receive the free gift of eternal life Jesus bought for him by His death on a cross.

It was a miraculous moment—God reached down into their circumstances. Through a pirated DVD of *The Passion* on a battlefield, one Jeff led another Jeff into a relationship with the living God.

The very next day, the two Jeffs were again on patrol together. As his buddy watched in horror, the new believer was blown up in an explosion.

He had been a Christian for less than 24 hours, but that day, he was in paradise.

And in the future, those two Jeffs will be together again... thanks to a miracle of God.

CHANGED LIVES

This movie is remarkable on so many levels, many beyond comprehension. It is, without a shred of doubt, truly a life-changing experience for those who have seen it. Many, myself included, are returning to their long-abandoned faith. We are resolving to elevate our lives to a higher standard. Then, there are those who did not have a faith of any kind and now are searching for it. We are choosing to embrace God instead of denying Him. We are on a quest for something other than human existence.

It is no coincidence that I feel a transformation underway as it has been 19 days since I was given the immeasurable gift of viewing the movie. There is a definite link between the two. In fact, I have seen it six times already. Each viewing opens my heart to Jesus a little bit more. I believe that God is reaching out to me as I watch this film. Am I to turn away from His message? Do I give the message I am receiving a deaf ear or a blind eye? Do I think that I am hallucinating and shrug the whole thing off? Do I deny Him like Peter? The answer is absolutely no!

I have denied and not believed long enough! My soul does not have the luxury of doing so any longer.

—Internet submission

Ten thousand sermons could not have impacted me in the manner that this film did. I have been a Christian since 1978, and nothing has been more profound in my life than this depiction of *The Passion of the Christ*. After viewing this epic, I understand why there was so much controversy surrounding this film: It is the truth, and most people cannot deal with the truth. In these last days, I thank God that He has used Mel Gibson to remind us of the price that our Lord and Savior paid for our redemption.

Peggy—Belleville, Illinois

I was raised in a Christian home. I have served in the church I attend and been on charity trips to some really forgotten places inside my country. But never have I experienced such a great impact about Jesus as after seeing this film. It really makes me think before doing something wrong. I feel more patience towards everyone. I feel the urge to love them.

But more than what has happened in my life was the experience an uncle of mine went through after seeing this movie. I won't tell his name, but he has always been reluctant to give his life to the Lord, and he even showed an attitude of indifference. I have always admired him because he is very intelligent and also a very good film critic. We used to spend long hours talking about films. But now he said he personally accepted Jesus as his Savior and is willing to confess it publicly in our church. This news in my life really makes me happy.

Jorge—Guatemala

I coordinate a support group for teen moms and dads (ages 15-22). We took a group of 16 young moms and dads to *The Passion*. I have been working with these teen parents for three years and *nothing* has impacted them as much as this movie. Afterward each one shared how much the movie impacted them. We prayed with some of these young parents and many told us how they've made a decision to follow Christ.

Since that time these teen parents have been reading their Bibles and are getting together with leaders to discuss their questions.

Their comments include:

I didn't even know the true story of Jesus' death. I've seen paintings of His crucifixion, but they showed His perfect body just hanging there—there are usually no marks to show His suffering. I know now that He suffered so much…for me.

—Lynsie

The movie was really hard to watch, but it made me realize that if Jesus hadn't gone through that then, I wouldn't have what I have now.

—Charlie

I want to see the sequel. And actually the prequel too. I want to know more about Jesus' life on earth and what happened after He was raised from the dead.

—Nate

The hardest part was watching Mary have to witness her son's suffering. Now that I'm a mom, it meant so much more to me.

—Mari

For it is by believing in your heart that you are made right with God, and it is by confessing with your mouth that you are saved.

ROMANS 10:10 NLT

Do not conform any longer to the pattern of this world, but be transformed by the renewing of your mind. Then you will be able to test and approve what God's will is—his good, pleasing and perfect will.

ROMANS 12:2

DOING THE RIGHT THING

TEXAS PASSION CASE

The day Jesus was crucified, there was a thief next to Him, also hanging on a cross. As he was dying, he mocked Jesus and taunted Him...cruel to the end. But there was another thief on the other side of Jesus, also being executed. This man was different—a criminal deserving death, yes. But in the final moments before that criminal's death, having witnessed Jesus' incredible passion—even for those who beat Him and nailed Him to a cross—this man came to see and believe that Jesus was the Son of God.

As this thief was dying, he asked Jesus one thing—would Jesus remember him when He got to heaven? In reply, Jesus spoke these memorable words, "Today you will be with Me in Paradise" (Luke 23:43 NKJV).

Our next story made national and international headlines. It's about a murder in Texas that the coroner ruled as a suicide, and the killer got off free and clear.

Perhaps.

Like the thief on the cross, this story is about another criminal who had a life-changing encounter with the Son of God.

CHANGED LIVES

January 19, 2004—the Fort Bend County Sheriff's office received a tragic call: a mother, Renee Coulter, had discovered her 19-year-old daughter, Ashley Wilson, dead in her apartment. A pillow case was over her head, and the cord from

her high school graduation gown was wrapped around her neck. It looked as though she'd hanged herself. But why?

Sheriff Milton Wright comes from a long line of Texas Rangers—the tough, legendary lawmen who helped tame the West. Wright had been in JFK's motorcade the day he was assassinated in Dallas, protecting then-governor John Connally. To say he's been around the block is an understatement. He's pretty much seen it all.

Sheriff Wright

We received a call to investigate a death. This one looked very cut and dry because of the way the whole situation played out. The evidence in the apartment suggested that there had been a suicide—the way the body was positioned, the door being locked from the inside, and a note suggesting suicide.

All the evidence pointed to suicide. A letter was found that could be interpreted as a suicide note. While it didn't actually say she was going to kill herself, it did state that she was extremely depressed because she was pregnant and the person she was pregnant by was not going to be there for her to raise the child.

Sheriff Wright

> With this evidence and other autopsy results, the medical examiner ruled the death as a suicide.

Despite the note suggesting suicide, Renee Coulter and her husband, Dan Wilson, had difficulty agreeing with the sheriff department's assessment. To them, the evidence just didn't add up to the person they knew as her daughter.

As reported in the *Houston Chronicle,* the fact that their daughter's television, lights, and ceiling fan were off disturbed the parents. "My daughter lived in an apartment by herself," Coulter said. "She always had the TV on, always had the ceiling fan on, and always had lights on." Moreover, Ashley's apartment key was missing from her key ring. "To me, that meant that somebody *was* there and had taken the key," Coulter added.

To the police, the response of the parents was perfectly understandable. A family in shock and grief. Suicide is hard to accept given someone so young and with all her life ahead of her. But after getting the report from the Harris County medical examiner that it was definitely a suicide, Sheriff Wright's office closed the case on Ashley Wilson.

Dan Leach is a 21-year-old young man who had been in a relationship with Ashley. That relationship had soured shortly before the time of her death, and some felt it was the motive for her depression and the sad letter she'd left behind.

Leach was depressed as well. He was a guy who went to a local church in the area, but he was a troubled and conflicted man.

He was also a murderer.

March 2004—Less than six weeks after Ashley's death, *The Passion of the Christ* came to Richmond, a small town outside of Houston. Like most other locations around the country, the theaters were packed as a result of all the buzz about the film. A young man bought a ticket and went into the theater for an experience that would change his life forever.

Shortly thereafter, that man walked into the Fort Bend County sheriff's office and turned himself in for the murder of Ashley Wilson.

The police were perplexed. That case was closed. Her death was a suicide. There was no murderer.

Dan Leach convinced them otherwise.

Sheriff Wright

When he came in, he was very, very cooperative and gave us explicit details of how he had planned the murder, committed it, and the things he had done nobody else could have known because the information was not public knowledge. He had to have been there because he had knowledge of what had gone on during the murder.

The authorities were stunned.

Sheriff Wright

The description of Dan Randall Leach would be an average American male. Prior military, graduated from high school, and, as far as I know, no criminal history.

Leach believed that Ashley was pregnant. That was his motive for killing her. She was pregnant and he was embarrassed and he wanted her totally out of his life.

It was a sickening admission.

And the surprises kept coming. What Ashley Wilson's former boyfriend, Dan Leach, had to say next to law enforcement would shock everyone. Seeing *The Passion of the Christ* had been a pivotal factor in Dan's decision to confess his crime.

In an exclusive interview with KTRH Radio in Houston, Leach revealed what was going on inside the mind of a murderer—and the miraculous conviction in his spirit that only an encounter with the living God could produce.

Dan Leach

I went and saw the movie with a couple friends. It was very intense, and having that visual stimuli really helps to focus; it does move you. After watching that movie I was very emotional. I thought about the things I had done, and I was upset that I hadn't repented yet.

Being guilty, I knew I couldn't repent to God for it and be forgiven spiritually without going to the law and allowing them to take their course of action.

In all of attorney Ralph Gonzalez' 24 years of law practice, this was something he had never seen before. He'd been a prosecutor and was now a defense attorney, but this was not something you find in law journals.

Attorney Gonzalez

At the present, I'm the court-appointed attorney to represent Dan Leach. He's accused of having murdered a lady here in Richmond, but that's not the unusual part. Murders occur all the time. I have prosecuted and defended several murderers.

This is a very unique situation for two reasons. First of all, I have a client who is professing his guilt, his complicity in the crime, but, most importantly, that he has a reason that he is doing so [confessing].

Dan had gotten away with the crime he committed. He allegedly had staged it as a suicide, and the authorities believed that it was a suicide.

According to Gonzalez, Dan Leach was also someone who believed in Christ, though clearly he was not following Him.

Leach was very ashamed for what he had done, and felt the incredible burden of guilt growing heavier and heavier.

Attorney Gonzalez

What makes this case most peculiar is the fact that this person had already gotten away with it, but he could not live with his conscience.

Just a couple of days after [committing the crime], his conscience began to eat at him and eat at him and eat at him. He became very ashamed, very disgusted with himself over the crime. He needed to tell someone; he needed to get back in God's grace. He wanted to do that, but he really didn't know how.

Dan struggled for about six weeks after the alleged crime. Then he went down by the river and prayed to God for an answer. He was torn; he already had gotten away with it and he wanted to get right with God. At that point in time, he felt that God spoke to him and told him: "Go confess."

It was in the midst of making the decision to confess his crime that Dan went to see *The Passion of the Christ*. There was no turning back. Experiencing the killing of an innocent man was more than he could take. Seeing the thief on the cross being executed, and knowing that he was going to be with Jesus in eternity, no doubt spoke directly to Leach's equally dire circumstances. He was compelled to come clean on the heinous crime he had committed—knowing full well that in Texas, they kill you for crimes like that.

When asked why he came forward now, Dan said that *The Passion of the Christ* had moved him spiritually.

Sheriff Wright

He had watched the movie *The Passion of the Christ*. His statement indicated that the film probably pushed him over the edge as to wanting to confess and clear his conscience.

Attorney Gonzalez

When he saw the movie, that was the very last thing. It was the last piece of the puzzle in his mind that moved him to go and confess.

He wanted redemption.

Before going to the police, Dan confessed his crime to the elders at his church and then further told the church that they will hear about a very heinous crime. He told them they will hear things about him that will disgust them and "that he is starting a journey that he doesn't know where it will end."

Dan

I knew I was wrong when I did it. I knew I was wrong in not going forward with it immediately. I knew throughout several occasions, when it came to mind, that I needed to do something about it.

I decided, before time ran out, before something happened to me, that I should go ahead and try to get on the correct path with God.

Once at the sheriff's station, Dan gave his confession to the police and they took him into custody, putting him under a $100,000 bond, which he chose not to make.

Sheriff Wright

When a murder is planned like this, almost all the time the perpetrator overlooks one minor detail, and like a thread on a piece of cloth, the crime starts to unravel from that point.

This one looked very cut and dry because of the way the whole situation played out. Had he not come forward and confessed, this one would never have cleared. People from time to time come and confess to crimes just to clear their consciences, but this is the first time ever in my experience that somebody has used a movie as a basis to give a reason for doing so.

At the time of Ashley's death and Dan's confession, investigators were unclear whether she had been pregnant or not. The state of Texas has one of the strongest laws in the country protecting unborn children from violence. There, under a law enacted in September 2003, the state defines an unborn child as "a person" and, by that definition, has the ability to charge someone with a capital murder for killing a mother carrying an unborn child.

What that means is that the crime is punishable by death, while a murder sentence carries a maximum penalty of life in prison. When Dan turned himself in to the police in March 2004, he could have been the first person prosecuted under the state's new law. He turned himself in knowing he was probably facing the death penalty.

However, since that time, the authorities have determined that in fact Ashley was not pregnant at the time of the murder.

So on March 22, 2004, a grand jury indicted Leach for first-degree murder.

Dan Leach had said that he was going to plead guilty in court to the crime. Attorney Gonzalez, in an effort to seek to "temper justice with mercy," pleaded "not guilty" on Leach's behalf in order to protect Leach's rights in the event of a trial. Gonzalez says that Leach admits to killing Ashley—there is no question as to whether or not he did it—by his own admission. But he is hoping to have an opportunity whereby a jury can encourage other criminals to turn themselves in by offering them a prison term of 20-30 years instead of life—or death. He believes there is always hope of redemption—only by God's hand—even in the case of a horrible murderer like Dan Leach.

It is a tough moral dilemma for Gonzalez.

Attorney Gonzalez

I only hope I can temper justice with mercy in the end. In 24 years I have become very familiar with jailhouse religion, where you acquire religion when you get to jail. It's obvious to me that this guy had religion prior to going to jail. The only bad part to all of this, and the one that troubles me the most as a criminal defense attorney, is if he was that moved by God to confess, what moved him to possibly commit this crime?

There's an anomaly there. You either love Christ or you don't. You've either taken Him into your heart or you haven't. It's not something you switch on and off...that's the grave issue for me.

But I don't judge my client; I represent my client. I believe that somehow, somewhere, someway he disconnected his head from his heart and did an act he's very, very sorry he committed, and now he's willing to face justice. I can only hope that, at the end of his days, God will take Dan under His wing and say, "My son, you did the right thing...you did the right thing."

On August 11, 2004, Dan Leach's trail began. Leach changed his plea to "guilty," stating, "I assume full responsibility for my actions."

Leach wept and displayed a tremendous sense of remorse in the courtroom as the jury was to shortly determine his fate. He told his attorney, "It doesn't matter what they give me."

Attorney Gonzalez told me, "He has more faith and courage than I do."

Two days later the jury pronounced the sentence: 75 years.

Twenty-one-year-old Leach will not be eligible for parole until 2041, when at least half of the sentence has been served. "Dan Leach got away with a perfect crime," said Attorney Gonzalez. "He got away with it, but he could not live with the fact that he took a human life."

God had changed a murderer's heart.

THE RESCUE

On a sunny Saturday morning in March 2004, 80-year-old Wanda did what she's done almost every Saturday for the last 23 years. She drove to a nearby medical clinic, to speak to young women on their way into the clinic for appointments.

The young women's intent is to end a pregnancy through abortion.

Wanda is there to try to lovingly persuade them that there is a better solution to the challenge the women are facing.

But what she saw this morning was unlike anything they'd ever experienced.

CHANGED LIVES

A middle-class white woman in her late twenties or early thirties approached the abortion clinic. She had an appointment. Wanda made her way over to her and offered some literature explaining some options the young lady perhaps had not considered. Like many, the woman refused to take the brochure and continued toward the door. Wanda pleaded and the woman relented, took the material from her, and went in.

Wanda prayed that the woman would somehow change her mind and decide to save her baby. But she knew from experience that very few turn back. She prayed as if the woman would be one of the few.

Others came and went, but about 20 minutes later, out walked this young woman whom Wanda had given the brochure to. She was elated to see her leaving so soon...not enough time had passed to perform the procedure.

The woman approached Wanda. She looked strangely calm and peaceful—not troubled as most women leaving the clinic appeared. Then she said the words Wanda longed for, "I'm not going to go through with it."

Wanda was curious. "Did anything we said have anything to do with your decision to not have an abortion?"

The woman replied, "No—that did over there." She then motioned toward a building situated diagonally across the street.

Wanda was puzzled. "I don't know what you mean."

The woman pointed at a movie theater. On the marquee two stories up were the words, *The Passion of the Christ.*

"You see that? *The Passion*...I looked out and saw that, and that's what did it."

Wanda stood there, speechless. She was stunned.

The woman then calmly walked away, never to be seen again.

Wanda says that in her many years of sidewalk counseling she's spoken with thousands of women, but she's never had an encounter like this before. "It was very exciting. I couldn't believe it when she said this. Sometimes they cry, but she was very calm...at ease...relaxed—relieved. That's the word. She looked *relieved.*"

Later Wanda realized what a wonderful miracle had taken place. The waiting room for the abortion clinic is on the second floor, and a window faces that theater marquee. The young woman had no doubt sat down and stared out that window directly into those powerful words, *The Passion of the Christ*. There may have been other seats that didn't face the window…the window shades might have been drawn. She might not have had time to reflect on those words at all.

But Wanda was praying for God to touch her. Somehow. And a miracle happened. "God works in strange ways—and that's very strange. She didn't even go in and see the picture—just the title! Sometimes just a sentence will change your mind. I suppose she thought about *The Passion*—all that Jesus did for us, and here I am about to destroy one of His miracles."

Wanda will be in front of some medical clinic this Saturday morning, praying for another miracle…and knowing those prayers are answered in the most unexpected ways.

CHANGED LIVES

I have always had a profound faith. It's what keeps me going on those days I feel as though there is nothing left. I need to tell my story on the seriousness of my reaction to this movie—it has changed my outlook on life in general.

I can't explain the sorrow I felt as I watched the movie. I was actually sobbing and started to weep uncontrollably. There was something inside of me that changed that afternoon; I felt so ashamed, as though I have wasted so many years on things that really didn't matter. I looked around at the people in the theater afterward and thought to myself, *What in the world have we done to our society?* We are clueless to what's really important. I felt angry—that we are beings of pettiness and destruction. I was not only emotionally drained, I was physically drained from the movie. I was upset at myself the whole night and didn't have words to say; I just kept asking for forgiveness. And I still cry when I think about Jesus on the cross asking for His father to forgive the men who crucified Him.

—Internet submission

Well, I have been a "Christian" for many years, but the past several no one could tell from my lifestyle. As a matter of fact, to make money I started a website that would be considered soft-core porn by some and nothing by others, but I was heading in the direction of adult entertainment for sure.

I went to see *The Passion,* and after seeing what Christ went through because of His love for me—a visual of what He paid for my salvation, and the "friend" He was—I had to close the site. It will be deleted from my servers within the next week. This movie touched me so much I took my kids and my friends' kids to see it, and one of them accepted Christ as her Savior afterward.

—Internet submission

I have been a Christian for about 20 years now. After watching *The Passion* I had a hard time getting out of my seat, let alone leaving the theater. Although only 7:00 P.M., I went to bed—with my Bible—upon arriving home. I have not stopped thinking and praying since. My encounters with everyone, good and bad, have been affected. Although I realize I am seeing the actor's face, they are Christ's eyes looking right into my soul as I now interact with others He has created and loves. And the flashbacks of just what He would do to allow me to have eternal life…*I will never forget.* At least, that is my prayer. I remember the disciples saying things they would never do and yet…

—Internet submission

For God so loved the world that He gave His only begotten Son, that whoever believes in Him should not perish but have everlasting life. For God did not send His Son into the world to condemn the world, but that the world through Him might be saved. He who believes in Him is not condemned; but he who does not believe is condemned already, because he has not believed in the name of the only begotten Son of God.

JOHN 3:16-18 NKJV

FREEDOM

THERE WERE THREE CROSSES

"The graphic display of hatred and love moved me. I realized there were many traits in my life I needed to change."

"I saw through a mother's eyes how I must let my children go through trials and tribulations."

"Had I been born at His time…I would have been drawn to Him to help Him when carrying the cross or when He was down, no matter the cost to myself because that is the kind of being I am."

Words all spoken from the heart.
From the hearts of hardened criminals.

CHANGED LIVES

The Saturday before Easter 2004 was a very special day for 250 women in south Florida. Of the 37,000 prisons in America and over a million inmates, they would be the first to see *The Passion of the Christ* in prison.

It would be a greater privilege than any would imagine.

Everyone knows that most prisons are very bad places to be in. They are filled with what many consider the rejects and refuse of society. Throwaway people. For women it can be particularly hard. You're lonely, separated, or even abandoned by family or those you had hoped would stand beside you. Women receive far fewer visitors than men. Male prisoners are more likely to be visited by girlfriends or wives and family, who often stick with them at least for some time. But when a woman is put in jail, most often the man in her life just disappears. She is on her own. And perhaps worst of all, she knows deep down that she has really messed up her life, and she can't undo what she has done.

Hope vanishes quickly. Desperation sets in.

It is the ideal setting for a miracle.

That's why Raeanne Hance, the executive director of Chuck Colson's Prison Fellowship Ministry in Florida, jumped at the opportunity to show *The Passion of the Christ* in the Broward County Correctional Institution. It's a maximum security women's prison filled with murderers, drug dealers, racketeers, robbers...you name it.

Jennifer Giroux, the founder of an Ohio-based women's advocacy group called Women Influencing the Nation, had been working in cooperation with Mel Gibson's Icon Productions to get *The Passion* into prisons. She and Raeanne teamed up and facilitated an unprecedented event with eternal consequences.

Raeanne Hance

Broward Correctional Institution is one of Florida's maximum security prisons for women, holding about 900 female inmates, some with life sentences. When word leaked out about this screening of *The Passion,* 90 percent of these women wanted to be there. This was such a special opportunity for these women, and all of us really believed that the message of this film would change hearts in this prison forever.

Getting the film into the prison was no small task. Mariam Bell, the director of Public Policy for the Wilberforce Forum, a division of Prison Fellowship Ministry, understood this well.

Mariam Bell

The prison environment is not like any other. You always have to take into consideration the potential risks involved with having large groups of inmates together and, in this case, having them in a room where the lights would be out. Naturally, there are a lot of hoops to go through on something like this.

Fortunately, Prison Fellowship Ministry has been working in Florida's prisons for a number of years now, and both the governor and the state's head of corrections were very supportive of getting the film into Broward. Even with this, given the tight time frame and the kind of practical logistics needed to be worked out, Warden Denise White decided not to reveal the possibility of the screening to the inmates until it was a "sure thing."

She knew these women had experienced a lot of disappointment in their lives and didn't want to risk them having yet another one. As a result of these various factors, the women didn't have an expectation about what was going to happen that day.

The women who were invited to see the movie had earned the privilege due to good behavior. Religious belief was not among the criteria for selection, so many religions and beliefs were represented among almost 300 women squeezed into every inch of the recreation room where the screening was to take place.

Danny Rafic, an assistant editor on the film and the representative from Icon overseeing the screening, had never been in a prison before and certainly not a women's prison! He definitely had some hesitations about it.

Danny Rafic

To be honest, being there scared the living daylights out of me! I thought I was going to be in a booth in the back, but here I am kneeling and crawling around, stringing cables, setting things up, surrounded by women who had committed murder or armed robbery. Some of their faces were so hard. I didn't want to make eye contact with them.

Yet, when they introduced everyone—including me—all the women said, "Hello, Danny!"...and my heart began to be touched.

Danny had shown the film dozens of times to special groups across America. But none of those experiences was like this. He was in for a great surprise.

The lights dimmed, and no one—not prison officials, Danny Rafic, MSNBC, or the local news media covering the event—knew quite what to expect. What happened next impacted everyone.

Raeanne

The inmates were very engaged with the film. During the first scene in the garden, when Jesus Christ crushes the snake's head with His foot, the women absolutely erupted with cheers.

Danny

Before going to Broward, I had shown the film at least 60 times. And in all those other audiences I had never seen anything like this. The women were very vocal; they hugged, cried, shouted at the screen. To me, the women were actually sharing in the pain they saw on the screen. I'd never seen anything like it.

When Jesus' trial was going on, they would talk to the screen—to Pontius Pilate and say, "Let Him go." And when they released Barabbas, they all yelled, "No, no! That's not right…"

Mariam

Remember that the audience at Broward was not the audience you'd find in your local movie theater. There is very little pretense among these women about the reality of their situation. Compared to many of us on the outside world who don't think our lives need much help, these inmates know the reality about their lives. Moreover, they know that you know it as well.

Danny

You could feel the tension building as we approached the scourging scene. As Jesus was taking more and more of the beating, taking on the responsibility for humanity, the inmates responded to the violence in such a profound way. As these women—many who have been in violent situations—watched Jesus being whipped, they wept as if they were actually the ones beating this innocent man.

Mariam

They didn't just sniffle during the film—they wept and sobbed at what they saw. Some were so completely overwhelmed that they had to leave the room for a time. One woman was helped out by guards—who were also crying. A short time later the woman returned saying, "I just couldn't take it…I couldn't take it…but I was the one who put Him up on that cross—so I came back—I *have* to see it!"

  I'll never forget that during the scene when Jesus is being brutally scourged, a number of the women started shouting and screaming, "Stop it! Leave Him alone!"

The women's responses to the film were quite unique. This was a most unusual audience—but perhaps it was simply  because their sins have a name: Crime. Assault. Murder. Robbery. Ours seem more benign as they usually don't manifest themselves in such a pronounced form, but they are just as damaging to our souls.

  And this is how these women prisoners are more perceptive and receptive to the truths of this film: They readily were able to identify the evil in themselves, and the evil in the world. Most interestingly—and this is why they all had such a profound emotional response to the scourging and flogging scenes—each of the women prisoners seemed to identify themselves either with Jesus—a victim who was being horribly abused, or with the Roman guard who was doing the abusing.

  Each of them had either been the abused or the abuser. And in many cases, both. Either way, they knew they needed healing. They were desperate for it.

  Perhaps one of the most powerful moments came near the end of the film when Jesus is being crucified between two thieves. Just before his death, one of the thieves comes to believe that Jesus is the Son of God, and he asks Christ to remember him when "You come into Your kingdom."

To this criminal paying the ultimate price of his deeds, Jesus responds with words of great hope, saying, "Today you will be with Me in Paradise." It is a powerful, emotional scene, and in most theaters the moviegoers are silent and very introspective.

But what happened at that moment in the prison stunned everyone.

The women leapt to their feet, cheering like fans at the game-winning shot at the NBA finals! Tears poured from their eyes as they shouted for joy! In that thief, those women could see themselves. They com-pletely identified with him. They knew they could be free. For the first time for the vast majority of them, hope entered their lives in that instant.

Jesus was dying, but they did not see death—they saw life. They saw hope. They saw the future.

Nowhere was this more evident than in the end of the film.

The resurrection. Life after death. Jesus arises and walks out of that tomb. I and the hundreds of other moviegoers in the theater sat in stunned, reverent silence. But for inmates with no future outside those walls, theirs was an entirely different experience.

Jennifer Giroux

There were violent criminals at Broward, and yet here was the first group of people I had ever seen cheer at the end of the film! All of the women literally stood up on their feet and applauded and cheered!

Raeanne

It was an amazing moment…this standing ovation. To me, it meant that this film had accomplished something priceless: It had given these women, these prisoners, hope.

After the film, Warden White had planned simply to get the inmates back to their cell blocks. But with a microphone in her hand, the warden decided to ask if anyone wanted to talk about what they were experiencing—and hands went up all around the room.

Danny

The most amazing thing happened as the women began to speak, one after another. They started to express regret and remorse for what they had done in their lives. You know, it was told to me that 90 percent of inmates in prison say they're not guilty—but these women stood up and took complete responsibility for what they had done. Those who had never admitted to any crime were standing up, weeping.

Danny observed that what he was experiencing was how one film accomplished in just over two hours what a lifetime of therapy might never have been able to do. The women clamored to tell their stories…to share how they had been impacted…to tell anyone who would listen that they had been changed forever…and say those things that high-security inmates just do not confess…

"I've done all this bad stuff in my life and this movie is gonna make me change. I am starting right now."

"I know I did wrong."

"I asked God for help, and this time I don't want to fool around. I want to do it for real."

"We have no right complaining how we are treated, the conditions here, after seeing how Christ was treated."

"I'm a murderer who made myself out to be innocent. After seeing how Jesus sacrificed for me, I know I'm not."

"I've been praying. There is so much going on in my life. Change is what I need. I don't want to be here. I want to be home with my children. I want to stay out and stay on track."

"I keep asking God, 'Show me what You want me to do in the free world [life outside of prison].' I'm giving my life to Him and I'm not coming back to prison."

"I am committing my life to Christ, and all of you need to do the same."

Danny

I found my heart breaking for these inmates, and I cried a lot. Although most of these women were guilty of things, I saw that they had come from broken homes, that they didn't have any support. They were alone. To see them break down and confess what they had done in life touched me so deeply.

They felt as though we had made this movie just for them. I can't express enough how appreciative they were that we "chose" them to screen the film in their prison. It was as though we had given them a great gift.

I never dreamt that I would have ever been given this kind of opportunity in my life. These women have had so much hardship, and we were able to give them hope. I left the film with a natural high. I immediately called Mel and left a long message for him, telling him what happened. This was the reason Mel made this film.

When it was all over, the inmates gone and the news crews wrapping up their gear, something happened which can only be described as God giving us a little peek into the way heaven works. Mariam Bell remembers exactly what transpired.

Mariam

I overheard a news reporter interviewing one of the prison guards. It came out that the prison guard had seen *The Passion* in a movie theater and had been praying to God, asking Him to someway, somehow, get the film into Broward.

At that moment, Mariam knew.

Of all the prisons in the nation, the fact that *The Passion* had managed to make its way into Broward was no accident. The prayer of an everyday prison guard who had a heart for those women under his care had opened the way for God to do an incredible thing. What Mariam, Jennifer, Raeanne, Danny, and all these women had just experienced was God reaching down into everyday circumstances and changing the outcome of those circumstances because someone was praying fervently.

That's exactly what a miracle looks like.

And it looks like that woman who left the screening, crying uncontrollably—but returning to see the rest of it as she felt personally responsible for what was happening to Jesus. And afterward confessing, "I am changing my life…I'm gonna get out of here and be different!"

That's a miracle.

It looks like Danny Rafic, who reflected on the experience saying, "As a Jew raised in Israel, I didn't know what Christianity was all about before this film. Now, I do."

That's a miracle too.

And the woman in prison who sees Jesus' death and resurrection in an entirely new light. "What gets me is this world thinks Easter is about bunnies. They put on nice bonnets and go marching around in parades. They go to church only once a year, and that's what they call Easter? No! I won't ever call it Easter after seeing this movie. How could I? It's the day we celebrate the Resurrection. It's Resurrection Day because the only innocent prisoner in the world was taken to death row, and He was nailed to a cross, the *most* painful, humiliating death a person could ever experience…"

She's experienced the miraculous hand of God in her life.

Yes, there were three crosses on Golgotha the day they executed Jesus. One of those thieves killed beside Christ is with Him in heaven today. And so shall be many of the women who experienced Jesus' passion for them in that lonely prison in south Florida, Resurrection weekend, 2004.

CHANGED LIVES

Testimonies from the Inmates
at Broward Correctional Institution

I was blessed to be chosen to see *The Passion of the Christ* at Broward Correctional Institution. The graphic display of hatred and love moved me beyond words.

I realized there were many traits in my life I needed to change. How I treat others on a daily basis in words and actions, from a smile to a frown, even the mumbles under my breath.

I also saw the forgiveness and patience I need to show and use more to allow my trust and belief that God will do what needs to be done for all concerned, that the ultimate good is not this moment but the end.

Most of all I saw through a mother's eyes how I must let my children go through trials and tribulations. Pain for them. Weep with them. But also be strong and encouraging—holding on to the love God has for them.

—Karen

The depiction of what our Lord Jesus Christ suffered for us changed my life. After 32 years of living iniquities, I am now a member of God's family.

In reading the Bible, it was hard for me to comprehend the torment Jesus suffered. *The Passion* made me realize what a gift was given to me and that no matter what hardships I may endure, God's love shall carry me through.

Today I know I am one of His children and there is a place for me in the kingdom of God because He gave His life so that I could be forgiven.

—Katherine

Seeing *The Passion of the Christ* was an answered prayer. Every time I called home, someone was there to share their feelings or view of the movie. It's an incredible movie that you *must* see. *No one* can tell you about it.

I'm a born-again Christian and was before seeing the movie. But the full impact of the movie made me realize I was taking my walk with Christ lightly. I took Jesus for granted, but never again. When I read my Bible about Jesus' death, it gives me a whole new meaning to the word "crucified." I used to doubt Jesus' love for me, but I now know it's real. Now if I do something wrong and I ask Jesus for forgiveness, it's sincere and from my heart. I use to say, "God forgive me." Now I feel bad when I do wrong. I'll never take Him for granted again when I do wrong. I feel like I'm crucifying Him over again.

You couldn't have given this movie a better title. I now know and feel I've experienced *The Passion of the Christ*. Although all my life I've been told Jesus loves me, this movie is what *really* opened my eyes and made me believe it wholeheartedly.

My family (especially my mom and friends) told me Jesus loves me. I came to prison and lost all hope and belief. Even in my walk it was shaky, but during and after the movie, I can proudly say after 36 years I BELIEVE JESUS LOVES ME/US!

Thank you so much, Mr. Gibson. I can't remember what one of your people said about the baby with Satan but I thought it meant "born into sin." It was/is the best movie I've ever seen and I've seen plenty of movies.

The Passion of the Christ—watch it! Save your life!

—Veronica

Having the opportunity to see *The Passion of the Christ* still humbles me.

To have everyone I know see it will be one of my determined goals. Seeing Jesus suffer so clearly made my spirit acknowledge the true price He paid for my sins, and I rejoice knowing He fully bore all that just for me, that I truly have a Savior who suffered so much so that He can and does stand with me before the throne of grace and mercy—His shed blood covers me with awesome sacrifice and power.

This movie helped me see more clearly my soul's humble surrender to my Savior.

—Laura

I believe in "obsessive love," as Mel Gibson calls it. I felt this is what our existence is all about and Christ was born to show us how it works. He said we can do all that He does. He showed us pure love, compassion, and forgetting of self for the sake of others.

My spirituality has taken a back seat for years. It has taken me almost 50 years to feel it again. The only way to be truly on the right path is through faith, hope, love, and forgiveness. I hope that it kicks in for people to come back to the true spiritual nature of things.

I loved the movie, and I love Christ.

—Bonnie

Jesus answered, "I am the way and the truth and the life. No one comes to the Father except through me. If you really knew me, you would know my Father as well. From now on, you do know him and have seen him."

JOHN 14:6-7

FADE TO WHITE

A very wise man said something to me a long time ago that I have never forgotten. I was in a bad place emotionally, hurting from a broken heart, and stuck in the quagmire. I knew there were things I could do to make my life better—but I wasn't doing them. Sound crazy?

Well, it *is* crazy. And you and I do stuff like that every day. There are better ways to do things, better ways to live, but we are stuck in our own muck, often feeling sorry for ourselves and living—no, *existing*—as though we are on a treadmill, going nowhere fast.

During that time in my "treadmill condition," my friend asked me this profound question: How much longer do you want to feel bad?

How much longer did I want to feel bad? I had an immediate answer: Not another day—not another hour. I was sick and tired of feeling bad.

That was the moment.

I just needed to hear myself say it. I was tired of my life as it was, and it was time to do something about it. So I did. I reached out to God and made the remarkable discovery that the entire time He had been reaching down to me. He had a miracle with my name on it.

How about you? Is there something in your life you are sick of? Have you had enough? Are you ready to have a better life? Are you ready to get the junk out of your life that is stealing your peace, keeping you from living a life that counts for something?

If your heart says yes, then I have great news for you: God has a miracle waiting for you!

The stories you've read here are all true, but far more importantly, they are stories of *truth*. Each of these people you've read about will gladly tell you that truth—a God who is real, personal, and who cares about you specifically—has changed their lives forever. That's what miracles are all about: God reaching down into our circumstances, touching our lives, and changing us forever. Do you want that?

I believe that as Jesus was breathing His last on the cross, He was whispering my name. "Jody...I am doing this for you..." He knew that 2000 years later, a little boy would be born in Shreveport, Louisiana, in 1956 who was going to need a Savior—a rescuer.

He knew that you'd be born too, and that you were going to need Him to reach into your life and perform a miracle or two. And He whispered your name with His last breath, just before He died on that cross.

He did it for me.

He did it for you.

The Passion of the Christ ends with a beginning. It doesn't fade to black like most films. It fades to white. The open expanse made for your new beginning.

This book ends with a beginning also—but only if you want it to. You can easily move from places of darkness in your life to a place of light. All it takes is a willing heart that says to God, "I need You. I can't do this alone. I don't want to do this alone. I am tired of life as it is, and I want Your miracles—I want to be a different person. I believe that what Jesus did—His passion for me—is all I need. Change me the way You changed the people in this book. I receive what You want for me, because I know You have my best interests in mind all the time."

I assure you that if you open the door of your heart just a little bit and ask Jesus to come on in, you will never, ever regret it. Your life will be changed forever.

Don't believe me? Then ask Sam Marte—the former God-hater. Or Anthony Scott, who is now friends with a man whose jaw he broke. Or Michael and Krista Branch, whose baby daughter is alive and well after drowning. Or Jan "Lightning Boy" Michelini…or Dan Goldberg, a Jew who now knows why Jesus lived and died—and rose again. Or dozens of women in that prison in Florida who will never be the same…the stories go on and on and on.

Where is your miracle?

What will be your story?

There is another chapter just waiting to be written.

ACKNOWLEDGMENTS

Special thanks to:

Jean Christen at Harvest House, for pursuing me and not giving up; Carolyn McCready, Editorial VP at HH, for making it all easy; and editor Hope Lyda, for taking all the pieces of the puzzle and fashioning them into a coherent and artful mosaic while walking me through this process at the speed of light and doing so with a great sense of humor.

Author/writer/co-warrior Eileen Chambers, who helped me restructure my TV program into a book, praying hard and pulling long, eye-blurring days because she listened to God and heard Him say, "Go."

Jennifer Giroux, tireless defender of truth and advocate of the film for her support and resources in telling the wonderful prison story.

My pastor, Jack Hayford, for his participation and teaching that has both formed and transformed me; Lee Strobel, one of the smartest and God-revering men I know.

Martha Cotton and Larry Reid, the skilled field producers of my documentary, who assembled many of these moving stories after acquiring the great interviews adapted to these pages.

Anne Sharp, the remarkable producer/writer who discovered most of these remarkable stories, fact-checked them, and pre-interviewed the key players, convincing the more timid to go on-camera and share their new life.

Ken Slater, Rod Spence, and Keith Rousch, the editors of my documentary, who originally pieced together the interviews in a fine, storytelling manner that made my work here much easier than it might have been without them.

Becca Groombridge, for her sensitivity to God's voice as she created the images of Jesus' Passion for my DVD and this book.

Mel Gibson, for stepping out and following God's call to create a no-holds-barred masterpiece that will touch lives for decades to come.

My mother, Barbara, who prays as if everything depends on God but works as if everything depends on us, for being my biggest cheerleader, encourager, and prayer warrior.

And my eternal thanks and gratitude to Jesus, the God-man, for that incredible price He paid so I might live an abundant life here and now, and in the future with Him.

I can only barely comprehend it. But *The Passion of the Christ* has helped.

ABOUT THE ARTWORK

When I produced the TV documentary "Changed Lives: Miracles of the Passion," I knew one obvious fact: The scenes from the movie were extremely moving. Those images portraying the real-life torture and execution of Jesus would be burned into people's minds for years to come. Never had there been such an accurate depiction of the horror of a Roman flogging and crucifixion.

I was able to license a few brief clips from *The Passion of the Christ* for the broadcast of the program, but for this book I faced a challenge—knowing that because the visual images of Christ's willing sacrifice were so impactful, I would need to go a different direction to capture the agony, the sacrifice.

I enlisted the talents of storyboard artist Becca Groombridge. Herself a Christian and one who was deeply moved by the film, I tasked her with creating some art that suggested the scenes from the last hours of Jesus' life as the Bible describes them. Both Becca and I had visited Israel at different times, and we knew the look and feel of the land and its people.

We will never really know the price He paid, but for me, having a visual reminder is something I need.

Often.

ABOUT THE AUTHOR

Jody Eldred is an award-winning producer and documentary filmmaker in the news and television industry who has worked closely with Peter Jennings, Diane Sawyer, and Oprah. He has covered stories across the globe, including the Persian Gulf War in 2003, and did the first high-definition shoots ever for CBS' *JAG* and *Navy NCIS*. He recently conceived and was executive producer of an acclaimed documentary about people whose lives were remarkably changed after experiencing *The Passion of the Christ*. Jody has been featured on *Good Morning America*, MSNBC, *The Hour of Power, Inside Edition*, in the *Los Angeles Times*, and in articles worldwide about this documentary which aired on PAX, TBN, and released August 2004 on DVD.

To learn more about Jody Eldred and the documentary, visit:
www.MiraclesOfThePassion.com

For information on booking Jody for speaking engagements, please contact him at:
ExecProducer@MiraclesOfThePassion.com
Or
Miracles of the Passion
13428 Maxella Avenue #626
Marina Del Rey, CA 90292

YOU'VE SEEN THE MOVIE,
NOW SEE HOW IT'S CHANGING PEOPLE'S LIVES...

This inspirational documentary captures the true stories of people who have been radically and miraculously changed by God as a result of having seen *The Passion of the Christ*, one of the most influential films of our time.

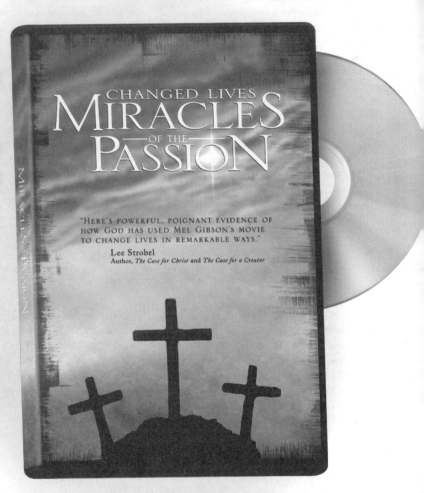

SPECIAL DVD BONUS FEATURES:

- Amazing night-vision footage of an audience watching *The Passion of the Christ*.
- Home videos of miraculous stories from across America.
- Top religious leaders' insights on *The Passion of the Christ*.

DVD
$14.95 OR LESS
S.R.P.

VHS
$9.95 OR LESS
S.R.P.

AVAILABLE WHEREVER VIDEOS AND DVDS ARE SOLD